EXPLORING NEW RELIGIOUS MOVEMENTS

Essays in Honour of

HAROLD W. TURNER

Edited by
A.F. Walls and Wilbert R. Shenk

on behalf of colleagues,
students and friends
in four continents

MISSION
FOCUS

1990

ISBN 1-877736-08-2

Printed in the United States of America

Published and distributed by
Mission Focus Publications
Box 370
Elkhart, IN 46515-0370 USA

Distributed in the United Kingdom by
Metanoia Book Service
14, Shepherds Hill, Highgate
London N6 5AQ, England

CONTENTS

FOREWORD

In every continent, there are people who are deeply thankful for the work of Dr. H. W. Turner. They include professional academics, for Harold Turner's contribution to scholarship is gratefully recognized by specialists in several disciplines. They include his former students (in New Zealand, Fourah Bay, Nsukka, Leicester, Emory, Aberdeen, and Birmingham), for he has been an inspiring classroom teacher and a valued research mentor. They include hosts of people in various walks of life who believe that their living, service, and understanding is better because he helped them to make sense of the cultural and religious situations in which they found themselves.

The contributors to this volume are representative of a vastly greater number who would wish to honour this great scholar in their work, and who unite in gratitude and good wishes to Harold and Maude Turner as they return to New Zealand for the next chapter of their remarkable story.

Harold and Maude Turner

A. F. Walls
University of Edinburgh

Building to last: Harold Turner and the study of religion

> By the grace God has given me, I laid a foundation as an expert builder, and someone else is building on it. But each one should be careful how he builds.
>
> PAUL TO THE CORINTHIANS (1 Cor. 3:10 NIV)

Harold Turner is the son of a builder and the father of an architect. His own knowledge of and interest in buildings is evident in his writings, and notably in one of his finest--and most neglected--works.

From Temple to Meeting House is about "sacred space," about the use by humans of buildings in recognition of The Holy, and as such it provides a starting point for considering the life work of its author. For as a scholar Harold Turner has been both architect and builder. He has recognized the need for certain types of scholarly construction and been a visionary designer of them. He has also been prepared to labour at the implementation of his designs, sweating with the bricks and mortar (not to mention the paint and putty) of scholarship. It has often been lonely labour, since some who might have helped were taken up with gaudy marquees that have long since collapsed. Turner's structures, like Noah's, have resisted the weather and, as the essays in this volume show, still invite habitation, adaptation, and extension--perhaps occasionally repair--for extended life in the climate of a new generation. Those who carry on the work of this expert builder may well remember *From Temple to Meeting House*. Turner's buildings are sacred space. They are designed not for spectacle, but for use; and they stand in recognition of The Holy. Unless this is recognized, their form cannot be understood.

A. F. Walls

At first sight his first book signals interests quite different from those reflected in the present volume, but it was a landmark in its way, and in many respects characteristic of its author. *Halls of Residence* was published in New Zealand in 1953, and, being speedily recognized as having more than local relevance, was republished by Oxford University Press the next year. It was the first, and perhaps is still the only, monograph on its topic. It arose from the experience of the author--he was also lecturing in Moral Philosophy at the time--in setting up student residences in what was then the University of New Zealand. It is informed by the conviction that student residences should express life in a community with a shared purpose and with shared values. Their purpose should be formative and in the fullest sense of the word, educational. It is one of the author's sadder literary memorials, for he has lived to see the conception of halls of residence, like their architecture, evacuated of that meaning so that their buildings decline into shacks for students.

By the time *Halls of Residence* appeared, Noah was being transformed into Abraham. Africa was drawing Harold Turner; but in those days there was no obvious route whereby a New Zealand academic could reach that land of promise. Harold and Maude, with a young family, set out for Britain to find one, and after a spell of teaching at Goldsmith's College, London, reached the critical point of their great migration. Harold was appointed to a lectureship in the Faculty of Theology at Fourah Bay College in Sierra Leone, the oldest university institution in tropical Africa. At that time affiliated to the University of Durham, it was in transition between the missionary institution it had lately been and the independent university of a new nation that it was soon to become. The Faculty of Theology was crucial in that transition. It had responsibility for the training of the ministry, at every level, for the country's three principal churches. It represented theology, no longer an acknowledged queen, in a consciously secularizing community. And it had to explore new religious frontiers locally, frontiers that Durham theology knew nothing about. Turner, commissioned to teach Biblical and Theological studies--naturally, he was a Warden of Students as well-- began by throwing himself into the first two of these tasks. They were an indispensable background for the third. In his contribution to a modest faculty publication celebrating Sierra Leone's independence he sets out a view of the theological task, and of the relationship of theology to other disciplines, which in developed form was to underlie much of his future work:

> ... a true knowledge of God the creator includes also a doctrine of human life and of the natural universe in which it is set. God cannot be known except through man and nature, and by this very fact both man and nature are seen in their unity and their meaning. Theology is the most concrete of all studies, since God, the creator and "constant environment" of all things, is the least abstract and isolated of beings. In former times this was recognized when theology was called "the Queen of the Sciences"; in some universities vestiges of this remain in the recognition of the faculty of theology as the senior faculty. ... [W]e at Fourah Bay College have no such ambitions; rather would we seek to serve all branches of knowledge by providing for their consideration a comprehensive framework within which all may find their place and their unity while retaining in full measure their own responsibility and freedom." (Sawyerr 1961:12-13).

There are hints here of later themes: the "mediated immediacy" in human encounter with the divine--an idea developed from a brief discipleship with John Baillie in Edinburgh; a view of theology as an integrative discipline; and yet the recognition of the autonomy of each academic discipline within its own sphere. This view of the totality of human knowledge and the freedom to increase it, within-- not supplementary to--a Christian confession about God and the world, is a keynote in his most recent thinking with its keen interest in modern scientific thought and in the historic dependence of scientific method as a Christian worldview. This declaration of the autonomy of academic disciplines has paradoxically irritated some of his critics because of its implied resistance to the subsumption of the whole study of religion under some other discipline (Wyllie 1980:81-92). The position he enunciates in this article is fully in the Reformed tradition in which he was reared--and Harold Turner has always valued the sense of identity, the freedom to be oneself, which comes from sharing in a tradition--and the combination of ultimate commitment and liberty of exploration has never left him. It has enabled him to enter sympathetically into cultures and religious--and non-religious--traditions not his own. It has opened him to insights from a variety of intellectual approaches, and his breadth of discourse has allowed him to place the results of his explorations on the general map of learning.

One day in 1957, on Lumley Beach near Freetown--a place for them of spiritual exercises--Harold Turner had met white-robed members of the Church of the Lord (Aladura) and their remarkable leader, Apostle Adeleke Adejobi. The encounter was to give Harold Turner's work a new direction and to release his richest creative activity.

It is worth remembering how little knowledge or understanding of the newer forms of African Christianity was then abroad. On the human level there were few situations where the old and new forms of African Christianity could meet on equal terms. In mission or "mainline" church circles the new churches were commonly regarded as "sects" or "cults," or as a syncretistic Cave of Adullam, frustrated ambition in league with polygamy, adultery, superstition, and ignorance. There were no widely recognized criteria for distinguishing one type of new church from another. The newer churches often denounced the older as powerless, mercenary, compromising with evil. Among scholarly writers Geoffrey Parrinder, as so often, was pointing the way, indicating in his study of religion in Ibadan the significance of the new churches (Parrinder 1953:107-132). But there were only two major studies generally available in English, and both were localized in reference. One was Bengt Sundkler's seminal *Bantu Prophets in South Africa*, then known only in its first (1948) edition. Sundkler revealed something of the size of that mass of Christianity outside the mission-related sphere and also something of its highly complex history. He uncovered indigenous religious initiatives little thought of beyond the Zulu domain, and set them in their local context. He also produced the first typology of the newer churches, distinguishing between their "Ethiopian" and "Zionist" forms. Sundkler wrote only of South Africa, where land deprivation and the sense of oppression were so intense; but others were soon finding parallels in the situation in other parts of Africa. The first academic work seriously to address the new churches in Nigeria--if we discount the section in Parrinders' *Religion in an African City* already mentioned--was by a political scientist (Coleman 1958). It invests them with a nationalist political significance which sits oddly on the great bulk of them. The other major study available--less well known and often hard to find--was Efraim Andersson's *Messianic Movements in the Lower Congo* which illuminated the thirty-year period from 1921 in which Simon Kimbangu and the movement deriving from him was the most notable but far from the only striking phenomenon. Andersson's word "messianic" became added to words already in use, such as "nativistic," "syncretistic," "prophetic," "separatist," and occasionally "millennial" or "chiliastic," to designate what churchmen and scholars alike were beginning to realize was a vigorous part of the religious scene in many parts of Africa.

Turner's new interest thus began at a critical time. "Independent churches," as they are now known, have rarely been a luxuriant growth in Sierra Leone, and the Church of the Lord (Aladura) was still a singular phenomenon in Freetown. Deepening acquaintance with it revealed both direct connections maintained across West Africa and parallels elsewhere.

The mode of investigation--and how crucial that was to all that followed--grew naturally out of the first encounter. He took his new acquaintance in the Church of the Lord seriously for what they were and for what they claimed to be: as fellow believers seeking to worship God and to experience the divine presence and power. This enabled him to build trust and friendship with Church of the Lord leaders and members and to share freely with them in their activities. This form of "participant observation" was not role play but deliberate sharing, as far as the participant was able, in what he took in good faith to be Christian worship by other believers. There was a shared ground in the acknowledgment of the Christian Scriptures, however different the traditions of use. So Harold Turner accepted the risks and the personal vulnerability involved in such openness. In return his new friends took him for what he was: neither as an outsider nor as a "convert" but as a fellow believer from beyond the circle of prophet-healing churches. Doors were opened to him in branch after branch of the Church right across West Africa.

This sort of ecumenism was not common in West Africa in the 1950s; certainly the resultant uninhibited participation of Apostle Adejobi and his cohorts in a Fourah Bay Clergy conference was something of an event. Throughout his career Harold Turner has acted as a bridge, a terminal which permits live contact. In one of the essays which follows Rosalind Hackett, representative of a younger generation of scholars, tells of her experience of being identified by the leader of another Nigerian independent church as "a spiritual daughter of the great Dr. Turner"--and this many years after his last visit there. She points out how many have followed his example in the simple act of taking the new Christianity seriously.

The first published fruits of the connection with the Church of the Lord were analyses and interpretations of liturgical documents, the church's litany and catechism. These studies were published in early issues of the *Sierra Leone Bulletin of Religion*, a small journal begun as a vehicle for the type of local studies now incumbent on the Faculty of Theology. Both have since been republished in two other places. They illuminated the way in which the new churches maintained continuity with the liturgical and the doctrinal traditions of the older churches--in this case the Anglicanism which had been the background of most of the aladura members a generation earlier--while re-ordering them and finding new elements to express notes in worship and catechism essential to them but missing from the Western liturgies. It was a first exercise in elucidating the continuity and new departures, the assumptions and the priorities of the new churches, the "spiritual" churches as they saw themselves.

The process was taken to a deeper level by an examination of the use of Scripture in the church. Turner worked steadily through the register of sermon texts maintained by the Church of the Lord. Contrary to what might have been expected of a body characterized by charismatic leadership, ecstatic utterance, dancing in worship, and individual revelations, the preachers of the Church did preach from texts and did regularly record them in a register. Turner checked one obvious possible source, the lectionary in the widely available *West African's Churchman's Calendar*--there was no obvious correlation, the texts were their own choice. The incidence of the texts indicated the parts of the Bible most in use, and the commonest themes of preaching and items thus helped to build a profile of the concerns of the Church. The outcome was *Profile Through Preaching* (1965). That this little book was published for the Commission for World Mission and Evangelism of the World Council of Churches indicates the growing consciousness in the older churches of the importance of understanding the indigenous African churches and of the inappropriateness to them of the norms of interconfessional debate developed in Western Christian history. The Church of the Lord, for example, used the Christian Scriptures and observed both dominical sacraments, two of the classic marks of the church in Protestant tradition. While the Apostle's Creed was certainly recited in services, there was a profound lack of interest in doctrinal concerns that had lain at the heart of Western agonizing; and an equally obvious concern with questions hardly raised in the West. It was the first of Turner's forays into the question of the frame of reference within which people in different cultures read the Scriptures, a topic on which Walter Hollenweger touches in his paper below. There are hints, too, in *Profile Through Preaching* of a wider possibility. What if the same method of analysis was applied to the preaching in other African churches? Are the outlines we can trace clearly and firmly in the indigenous African churches simply the contours of an African Christianity which is discernible as a substratum in the older churches, too? Are the older and the new churches converging? David Shank's paper on the spiritual itinerary of African Christians has much food for thought.

But at this time Harold Turner was concerned with plotting the contours of the Church of the Lord (Aladura). Though the articles flowed, the full published form did not appear until 1967. It is his magnum opus, or rather, magna opera, for--despite some confusion engendered by the cover and title page--it is two books rather than one. *History of an African Independent Church* is important not only as a detailed history of the Church of the Lord in four countries but for the insight it gives into the story of the whole Aladura movement. "Even now, thirty years later, the oldest churches know so little of the inner spiritual history of this great religious upheaval in their midst," writes Turner of a time in the 1930s (Turner 1967:26). What he describes is just that--an inner spiritual history with a very specific context, agony and ecstasy, yearning and fulfillment, controversy and consensus, triumphs and disasters of the sort well known to the student of conventionally prescribed church history; but occurring not in the Hellenistic Mediterranean or Renaissance Europe but in the Nigeria of the influenza epidemic and the post-war depression, with taxation a burden, disease a peril, several generations of decent Anglican Christianity and a less-than-half-comprehending and periodically jumpy colonial administration. The second, larger volume of the duo explores the whole range of the life and faith and manners of working of the Church of the Lord (Aladura). The two works taken together still probably provide the most comprehensive picture we have of any African Christian body of any sort. As far as the "spiritual" churches were concerned they were soon usefully supplemented by John Peel's more sociologically orientated *Aladura*, which appeared soon after (Peel 1968).

Meanwhile, Turner had become involved in matters concerning the new churches more widely, and especially in clarifying and fixing terminology. The Commission on World Mission and Evangelism sponsored a consultation at Mindolo, Zambia, in 1962, the report of which appeared with the significant if slightly clumsy title, *African Independent Church Movements* (Hayward 1963). Turner's contributions to the report are the bibliography and the first of a long series of his characteristic typological charts and flow diagrams. The report signals recognition in the wider church that Africa had churches--not just sects or cults--outside and beyond those hitherto accepted in Christendom. They were of different types but had in common that they were "African independent" churches, over against the "older" churches of Christendom, the sources of the missionary movements which had first brought Christianity to most of tropical Africa. At the same time, the independent churches were formally part of a series of movements indicating the interaction between African societies and the Christian faith, which itself could not be separated from the wider impact of the West; and the relationship of these movements to the Christian faith greatly. It was necessary thus to regard the flux as well as the forms. Both forms and flux are recorded in Turner's chart. It is the first version of his typology, which he was to refine over the years, and which necessarily included the terminology adopted at the consultation. The key term adopted there, "independent churches," (divided, as by Sundkler, between Ethiopian and Zionist, with Aladura added to the latter) has, despite some grumbles, been generally adopted. Rosalind Hackett's article shows that flux continues; the aladura are no longer the "new" churches of Nigeria, and some extension of categories is needed to cope with the dynamic ebullience of religion in today's West Africa.

Harold Turner's move to a post at the University of Nigeria Nsukka assisted the broader application of his work. Eastern Nigeria was a forest of independent churches of the aladura type, but mostly smaller, more localized, and less hierarchical than the Yoruba-originated Church of the Lord. Eastern Nigeria had had its own separate religious history, and its own prophets; and the government archives at Enugu provided new light on the Elijah of the Niger Delta, the one-time Anglican catechist Garride Braide. A whole long wall of the Department of Religion became devoted to a map whereon, as it was identified, was indicated the location of each congregation in Eastern Nigeria. The questions grew with the clusters of color-coded pins. Why were there 331 pins (mostly white for independent) in an area marking five miles from the centre of the middling town of Uyo? An extraordinary Mennonite missionary living near Uyo became the kindly Socratic midwife for a range of developments in relation to Uyo's burgeoning religious life. Mild, venerable, and not at all academic, Edwin Weaver, instead of instituting a new denominational church, had concentrated on personal relationships with and service to Ibibio independent church leaders. He also sought mutual understanding between the main representatives of the other churches of the area. With Harold Turner as consultant and facilitator Uyo became the scene of a regular and active study group with a most variegated set of participants, which stimulated research as well as reflection.

The University of Nigeria saw itself as a national institution in a religiously plural nation, and had a Department of Religion rather than of Theology. Within this, Harold Turner was responsible for teaching a course on the forms and history of religion. It drew him back to the study of religious phenomenology, and he drank deeply from Continental wells. He was to make his own contribution to the literature on phenomenology (the systematic study of the history of religion, as W. Brede Kristensen called it) but the phenomenology of religion also became an essential part of his regular tool kit in the area of study where he was now well known. He did not abandon his vocations as theologian and historian but took up a new one as well. The whole history of religion and its manifestations typologically considered became his intellectual grid. His established interest in typology, his long concern with the distinctive features of the Christian faith, the ponderings on Semitic religion and prophetic religion derived from his years as a teacher of Old Testament studies, all assisted the development. The phenomenological method had not been widely used in the study of African religion, still less in that interaction of Christian and African traditions to which his special studies had brought him. It is appropriate that this volume contains an essay from a German colleague of those days, Hans-Jürgen Greschat, who was already engaged on the same path.

Phenomenology has been sadly neglected in the English-speaking world, especially Britain where it has often been reduced to a survey of methods and approaches to religion. When he left Nigeria, Harold Turner seized the opportunity to initiate the study of religion at the University of Leicester. His successor, Peter McKenzie, tells below how Harold conceived a department built round the study of the forms and history of religion, of the triumph of the conception and its subsequent withering from the cruel winds currently blowing across Britain from Philistia. Later Harold was to teach phenomenology at the University of Aberdeen (since ravaged by the same blasts); and when quite recently he devised a syllabus for the Birmingham Diploma in the Study of New Religious Movements, phenomenology as a necessary tool for such study became a fixed part of the syllabus. It is significant also that teaching the subject led him to produce (Selbstverlag) an abridgement of and commentary on Rudolf Otto's *Idea of the Holy* which has made that work accessible to hundreds of students who--by this writer's experience--rarely otherwise get beyond chapter three. And we have already noted his major study of sacred buildings in the different religious traditions, *From Temple to Meeting House.* (As in *The Rise of Silas Lapham*, the title indicates direction of the story).

Phenomenological method brought new zest to his studies of what he has described as the relations of the new religion of Africa with the old. Historians of religion have always tended to centre on the "great" traditions of Asia and the Semitic world. But it is the primal religions, so often miscalled primitive, which underlie all the others and frequently give the clearest models of religion. Further, the clear historical relationship of the primal religions with Christianity gives them special claim to sympathetic historical study. Harold Turner's visiting appointment to Emory University, following the Leicester and preceding the Aberdeen years, gave him two years to study Native American religions, Native American Christianity, and the interactive movements (so different in their effects from those in Africa) between Christianity and the North American primal religions. His booklet, *Living Tribal Religions* (in a series mainly for schools, and therefore often overlooked) in which the primal religions are presented in terms of patterns of revelation and response, is a little classic of its kind. The present volume fittingly includes a contribution on primal religions in Harold's own native land, and its peculiar relation to Christianity, by his compatriot and former student, James Irwin.

But perhaps most important of all, his new involvement in the broader synaptic treatment of religion took Turner from *African Independent Church* to *New Religious Movements in Primal Societies*.

It is by his work on new religious movements, especially those in primal societies, that Harold Turner's name is most widely known. Many fine scholars have worked in parts of this field and produced superb studies of those parts; but more than any other one person Harold Turner has defined the field, surveyed it worldwide, identified the materials, and established the area as having a distinctive place in the study of religion.

Behind the concept lies Turner's continuing concern with the relation of form and flux. The interaction of mission-organized Christianity, other modernizing influences, and African traditional society produced a range of movements of which independent churches were not the only, but were certainly the characteristic, form. Parallel processes elsewhere--in Melanesia for instance--produced an equally luxuriant growth of new movements, but relatively few independent churches. New Zealand had a history all its own, with a large Maori movement beginning outside the Christian faith but becoming progressively more like a Christian church, while another movement which began as a Christian revival moved for a time in another direction. The Native American peoples, north and south, have a history of interactive movements; so do many widely separated parts of Asia; there are even one or two in the records of the remaining recent primal peoples of Europe. On this larger map, the typology Turner had used for his early work on African churches was revised and refined. There have been several versions, and we

A. F. Walls

have probably not seen the last one, but in general there are four main classes of movement in a spectrum from the old religion to the new: neo-primal, synthetist, Hebraist, and independent church. But it is of the essence of movements that they move; the dynamic components within them may draw them now further toward one end of the spectrum, now to the other.

Turner's working definition of new religious movements, in the form in which it appears in a celebrated article in the *Encyclopedia Britannica*, is:

> ... a historically new development arising in the interaction between a tribal society and its religion and are of the higher cultures and its major religion, involving some substantial departure from the classical religious traditions of both the cultures concerned, in order to find renewal by reworking the rejected traditions into a different religious system (Turner 1974:698).

In principle, therefore, new religious movements can arise from the interaction of any religion from outside upon a primal society. In practice, as the article goes on to argue, Christianity has been infinitely more productive of such movements than any other faith, whereas Islam, often present within the very same societies, produces next to none. Lamin Sanneh has an essay in this collection which may throw light on this.

Turner's definition--and the precise form here may bear the marks of editorial policy--has given rise to plenty of discussion. Those concentrating on one particular religious situation may be more impressed by the adaptive capacities of indigenous traditions and thus stress continuity rather than new creations (compare Janet Hodgson's article below). Those concerned with a general social theory of religion may wonder why the definition is framed in terms of primal societies--the early typologies of "revitalization movements" such as those of A. F. C. Wallace had a much wider reference (Wallace 1956); or they may question the meaning of "historically new"--in practice Turner's examples begin in the sixteenth century, though most are from the nineteenth or later. Church historians may similarly discuss whether "new religious movements" so defined really do introduce any fundamentally new element into Christian history. Was second-century Phrygian Montanism, for instance, different in kind, either in its manifesta-

12

tions or in the conditions which produce it, from many "new movements" today? Missiologists may ask whether any successful cross-cultural transmission of Christianity does not involve "some substantial departure from the classical religious traditions of both the cultures concerned, in order to find renewal by reworking."

All these may be points for discussion. They do not in the least affect the usefulness of the definition, for it marks the boundaries of a field which everyone must recognize consists of cognate items.

It is at this point that one of Harold Turner's most remarkable achievements begins. So far we have seen the architect of the study of new religious movements. But he has also been its master builder. Over the years, by hard travel--often involving a heavy programme of lecturing, conferences and other duties into which the literary quest had to be packed--intense application, and insatiable curiosity, he has assembled a massive corpus of material relating to new religious movements in every continent, in a multitude of languages, and in every conceivable genre. He has recognized that in this field the scrap of information or comment in a newspaper or missionary magazine may be just as revealing as a learned article. So he must capture the newspaper, the magazine, and the learned article. From this ocean of literature he has distilled a series of scholarly, annotated, user-friendly bibliographies. When it appeared in 1967, the *Bibliography of Modern African Religious Movements* which he prepared with Robert Mitchell seemed vast; when ten years later the first volume of his series *Bibliography of New Religious Movements in Primal Societies* appeared, we learned how much more there was in the girnal. And that represented only a selection from a still larger collection, and the quantity of material collected since 1977 is fiercesome. Turner's bibliographies are the starting point for any serious student of the new movements, and a reference point for anyone enquiring into many an aspect of African or Native American Christianity. It is understood that the long-awaited volumes relating to the rest of the world (including Latin America, which poses special bibliographical problems) are to be with us before long. Others have often been provoked to bibliography by Harold Turner, and this collection contains a bibliographical essay by a former student of his, Joseph Chakanza.

A. F. Walls

A conventional scholar would have considered his work for posterity done with the bibliography, and might legitimately reserve the actual materials gathered with such labour for his own ongoing researches. Harold Turner determined to make his whole collection, the literature itself, available and accessible. In the first instance it was to be available in a centre specifically dedicated to the study of the movements. But he also wished it to be available throughout the world, available above all to those in Africa and Asia and Latin America and Oceania whose religious history the materials reflect. And he wished it available without long journeys, or costly technology, or high-priced multi-volume sets which only major libraries could afford. Hence the painstaking investigation of various intermediate technologies and the laborious establishment of a sort of cottage industry which makes the corpus available in modest microfiche form and distributes it worldwide. Harold has insisted that the material properly belongs to the people of the areas whose religious activities produced it. The most invidious colonialism of our day is the colonialism of information, the establishment by large Western agencies of proprietary rights over it, the fencing of it round with logistical or financial barriers. In this matter Harold Turner has always been a pugnacious anti-colonialist.

All this required sustained vision and sustained toil. The large foundations and the learned establishment did not soon warm to the idea of such a Centre for the Study of New Religious Movements, and several noteworthy locations lost the opportunity to become the base for exciting developments. Peter McKenzie tells an early part of the story here, before the Centre--as the Project for New Religious Movements in Primal Societies--found a traveller's tent in the Department of Religious Studies at Aberdeen and then a safe home in the Selly Oak Colleges (from meeting house to temple?).

In the early days of the worldwide paper chase, Harold was usually alone in the work--no, never alone, for Maude sailed cheerfully into the quest as she had into all the earlier ones, whether they involved transporting a family or entertaining prophets (and other angels) unawares. For the establishment and maintenance of the Centre, Maude has always been ready to acquire what few skills she did not already possess. Aberdeen brought the energy and sharp eye of Jocelyn Murray to the project. Gradually a miscellaneous corps of volunteers emerged, from very diverse sources, to bind, to file, to pack, to translate--one aspect of Harold's plan for general accessibility of the materials was that key items in languages other than English should be translated.

It is safe to regard the Centre for New Religious Movements as one of Harold Turner's enduring memorials. The collection now has a safe haven. Harold has been able to hand over directorship to Dr. Jack Thompson (who contributes a paper here) with the assistance of Dr. Stan Nussbaum and an expert staff. Some far-sighted agencies recognize the benefits which the Centre can bring. The collection continues to grow, the field itself continues to grow--as Professor Parratt's documentation in this collection of a piece of recent Malawian history will remind us. The new movements cannot be ignored by theologians, a point strongly made in Carl Starkloff's essay. As for missiology, it will be evident to any reader of Wilbert Shenk's article that the movements open up a whole new frontier in understanding the impact of the Christian message on the world.

Towards the end of the sojourn in Aberdeen Harold Turner had another encounter which recalls the meeting on the beach in Sierra Leone three decades earlier. It led him into engagement with post-Christian religious movements in the West. There is no space to talk of what has followed, the defense of vulnerable groups and the activity on behalf of religious liberty. We note only that the Centre he founded is no longer the Centre for the Study of New Religious Movements in Primal Societies, but the Centre for New Religious Movements.

For Abraham has lifted his tent pegs and is on the move again. The last few years have seen his intellectual concerns, so long concentrated on cross-cultural situations, revert to the place of the Christian faith in the great non-Christian culture of the modern West. It is fitting therefore, that our collection includes a contribution that relates to this theme, by Harold's one remaining colleague at Aberdeen, James Thrower. In Harold Turner's concerns as he now returns to his homeland we hear some of the notes that sounded out in earlier years, including that Fourah Bay manifesto of 1961, but with a sonority that comes from all that has happened in the intervening years. The expert builder is still at work, and we may expect to see new walls rising.

A. F. Walls

His buildings have always been such as other people may live in and adapt for their own needs; indeed, he has always welcomed others to join him on the site, where Maude would never be far away with refreshment. Nor, rigorous scholar as he is, has he restricted that welcome to professional academics; he has known how much of the knowledge and skill required are in other hands. The contributors to this volume are merely representatives of a host of his associates from different periods and places who are in debt to his inspiration, his assistance, and his achievement. They are well aware that the best tribute they can pay the expert builder is to take care how they themselves build.

REFERENCES
Coleman, J. S.
    1958   *Nigeria: Background to Nationalism*. Berkeley: University of California Press.
Hayward, Victor E. W., ed.
    1963   *African Independent Church Movements*. London: Edinburgh House Press for World Council of Churches.
Parrinder, Geoffrey
    1953   *Religion in an African City*. London: Oxford University Press.
Peel, John D. Y.
    1968   *Aladura: A Religious Movement Among the Yoruba*. London: Oxford University Press.
Sawyerr, Harry, ed.
    1961   *Christian Theology in Independent Africa*. Freetown: [Faculty of Theology, Fourah Bay College]
Turner, H. W.
    1967   *History of an African Independent Church*. Oxford: Clarendon Press.
    1974   "Tribal Religious Movements, New," *Encyclopedia Britannica*, 18.
Wallace, Anthony F. C.
    1956   "Revitalization Movements," *American Anthropologist*, 56.

Wyllie, Robert W.
    1980   "On the Rationality of the Devout Opposition," *Journal of Religion in Africa* 11 (2), 81-92.

A. F. Walls

Hans-Jürgen Greschat
Marburg University

"The founder" of prophet movements and the phenomenology of religion

This essay is written to honor Harold W. Turner, the distinguished researcher, historian of religions, and author of pioneering studies. Turner is the enthusiastic inspirer who has put many younger researchers onto the right track and made them drive on full of zeal. He is the inventive facilitator who never tired of making his archives of source materials ever more extensive for others to use and of undertaking the laborious task of publishing bibliographies which assist researchers everywhere.

Whenever Harold W. Turner's name is mentioned, the study of new religious movements comes to mind. New religious movements--sometimes called other things--appear to be the Cinderella of the study of religions, with the happy ending still out of sight. Historians of religions are trained to choose as their favorite subject what some of them term a "high" religion. The opposite are thought to be "primitive" religions, and among these are a good number of new religious movements. The choice of so many scholars has to do with their trade. Philologists may feel ill at ease with a religion lacking written documents; their craft culminates in discoveries of originals, of proto-texts. The original form is thought to be the pure, orthodox expression of a religious doctrine. New religious movements more often than not oppose some orthodox creed. Many of them can even be said to be syncretistic, a word with a scarecrow effect for many.

Still more obstacles bar the way into the academic study of religions. Some scholars tend to represent a religion as if it were a school of philosophy, a system of ideas, an -ism. Such systems are arranged into manageable scholarly units to be studied and examined. They can even be mastered in due time, as the numerous experts for such -isms prove.

To specialize in one thing means to ignore other things. No religion is made up merely of a system of thoughts, of dogmatics. The study of new religious movements can warn those experts of -isms not to underrate what they leave out. The fact is that religions can and do exist without dogmatics. A religion lives as an organic unit or not at all; it is cut up into parts and particles by Religionswissenschaft only for the sake of academic study. As for change, neither a religion as a whole nor any one of its parts remains as it is forever. They change and keep changing. No such thing as a religious -ism exists in real life.

The door of the study of religions has been unlocked to new religious movements with the guard-chain still in place. On the other hand, the door of the study of society was opened all the way. Much seems to be easier in that arena. Sociologists limit their research neither to written documents nor to the orthodox. They study how cultures clash and how they mix. They come across social change every day. Small wonder that sociologists and social anthropologists outnumber other specialists in bibliographies of new religious movements. They stimulated most effectively the study of our subject. But social scientists have their own questions to answer. They turn to new religious movements, as a rule, not because these are religious but because they are movements moving masses, moving them to protest. Social scientists explain new religious movements as social phenomena. It remains for Religionswissenschaft to unfold their religious element.

The disdain of dominant scholars for unsettled, for undogmatic, and for recent religious manifestations makes them blind to what they are missing. Let me quote as evidence a particular piece of writing, selected for good reasons: it was published worldwide, was ignored almost 70 years and, last but not least, its author was Rudolf Otto who was much appreciated by Turner. His book *Das Heilige* was first published in 1917, reissued up to 44,000 copies, and translated into many languages.

In this work, Otto discusses the holy and how it becomes manifest. Our faculty to recognize such manifestations he calls "divination." The holy can appear in a human being. Such a person radiates holiness. But there are also fakes. Those who watch and listen must find out the truth for themselves. Without the divination of Jesus' followers, for example, Christianity could not have come into existence. Otto then goes on to say:

> Misapprehension of this is only possible if, attempting a one-sided approach to the phenomenon of the origin of the Christian Church, we try to reconstruct the facts solely by the methods of scholarship and out of the material afforded by the staled feelings and blunted sensibility of our present-day artificial civilization and complex mentality. It would be an advantage if, in addition to these methods, an attempt were made to frame a less abstract intuition of the genesis of original and genuine religious communities with the aid of living instances of the thing as it may still be found today. It would be necessary for this to seek places and moments at which even today religion shows itself alive as a naive emotional force, with all its primal quality of impulse and instincts. This can still be studied in remote corners of the Mohammedan and Indian world. Even today one may come upon scenes in the streets of Magodor of Marrakesh, which have the strangest outward resemblance to those recorded by the Synoptic Gospels: 'holy men' (and very queer specimens they generally are!) now and then make their appearance, each the centre of a group of disciples, and about them the people come and go, listening to their sayings, looking at their miracles, observing how they live and what they do. Bands of adherents gather round them, more loosely or more closely united as the case may be. 'Logia,' tales, and legends form and accumulate; new brotherhoods arise or, if already arisen, extend in widening circles. But the centre of it all is always the man himself, a 'holy man' in his lifetime, and what sustains the movements is always the peculiar power of his personality, the special impression he makes on the bystander (Otto 1969:157f.).

Nowadays, those looking for contemporary examples of how religious movements come into being do not have to wait to come upon some by chance. A fair number crystallize around some person of the kind Otto had in mind. Such individuals should be relevant enough to be studied by Religionswissenschaft. Let us have a look and see how far research has come.

Historians of religions investigating the beginnings of an individual movement will take all possible causes into account: cultural, political, historical, psychological, economical, geographical. They must, of course, not neglect the religious element and must explore and try to understand and explain it. But they cannot isolate the religious and present it out of its context. This is what the comparing student of religions seeks, to get at the purely religious, what is left after all layers--individual, cultural, historical--have been stripped off.

Those specializing in the phenomenology of religion should be interested the most in samples of what they term the "sacred person." Did phenomenology of religion and new religious movements ever really meet? A look into three monographs can tell. They are textbooks read and reread by generation after generation of German-speaking students to this day. The authors in their time have taught a few thousand students each in Dutch, German, and Swedish. A fair number of those students are by now teaching others in schools and universities. No doubt, these are standard-setting texts written by standard-setting authors.

Gerardus van der Leeuw's *Phänomenologie der Religion*, a classic, was first published in 1933 and was translated into English and French. Van der Leeuw taught History of Religions at Groningen. As a phenomenologist he was attracted by what was then called "primitive" by high religions. He depicts the holy men Rudolf Otto writes about as representatives of "sacred power," as "speakers," and as "founders." He quotes sources from ancient Israel, ancient Babylonia, ancient Greece and Rome, ancient Scandinavia, early Christianity, early Islam, Zarathustra, and Mani. He cites authors like Plato and Plutarch, Goethe and Richard Wagner. He does not leave aside primitive religions and refers to a possessed Melanesian, to how a prophetess is made on the Indonesian island of Buru, to what a "primitive" Toradja of Celebes has said. A reference to Blumhardt of Bad Boll, a Christian healer who died in 1880, covers modern times.

The second book, *Erscheinungsformen und Wesen der Religion* (1961), was written by Friedrich Heiler who taught history of religions at Marburg. He cites numerous instances of what the names "prophet" and "prophetess" stood for in religions of antiquity: in Syria, Asia Minor, Canaan and Israel, China, Greece, and ancient Germany. The Hebrew Bible, of course, particularly molds the image of prophet. Heiler found more instances in the New Testament and in the history of Christianity of early, medieval, and Reformation times. Turning to foreign traditions, he points out Zarathustra, Mani, Muhammad, even Gotama Buddha, who appears to have been prophetic to a certain degree. Nichiren, the Buddhist prophet of medieval Japan, is not forgotten. The author mentions primitive tribes and shamans in passing. He includes the present and names as prophetic figures of the twentieth century Professor Wilfred Monod, a Huguenot minister, and Professor Nathan Söderblom, a Lutheran archbishop.

Religionsphänomenologie (1969), the third textbook, was originally written in Swedish by Geo. Widengren who taught history of religions at Uppsala. The German translation, he says, turned out to be "almost a new opus." Widengren quotes the standard examples of prophet from the ancient Near East, from ancient Egypt and Greece, from the Hebrew Bible. He then calls to notice "forms of prophetic inspiration" among North American Indians. Unfortunately, he does not take up this matter he had come across reading "Prophecy, American" in Hastings' *Encyclopaedia of Religion and Ethics* (Spence 1919:381-82). In that article Lewis Spence mentions, among other Indian prophets of modern times, Wovoka, the Ghost Dance, and Mooney's classical monograph.

This is, as far as I can see, the closest any one of the three phenomenologists has come to new religious movements. None took up Rudolf Otto's lead, none felt stimulated to study directly what is termed "prophet" and "founder," to come face-to-face with some "queer specimens" of today's holy men and women. Rudolf Otto, who had founded the Religionskundliche Sammlung at Marburg, a museum for students to study religions with their eyes, was seeking vividness, evidence alive and whole. Scholars prefer the safety of their texts even if these present a religious article only as fragmented and long, long ago. If we want things to change somewhat, we should find better ways for students of religion to follow Rudolf Otto's counsel to look at what is before our very eyes.

Phenomenology begins when something appears. Van der Leeuw gave it a name. What kind of name could we give a religious phenomenon? Ideally it would be a new one that does not provoke associations stored in people's memories. Technology and the sciences invent their own names. Capra ibex or Laser may not be understood by everyone, but what they name could hardly be taken for something different.

Phenomenologists of religion select names already coined and in circulation. They borrow from two treasuries. One is the wealth of everyday speech. "Founder," for example, comes from there. Within a religious context it may be misinterpreted by someone recalling an acquaintance who founded a newspaper or a tennis club. Religious founders, as a rule, do their founding differently. To mark the difference, some phenomenologists add "sacred" to the word "founder."

The other storehouse is religion, European religion more often than not. The Greek word "prophet" translates the Semitic *nabi*. We name contemporary Africans or Polynesians or American Indians "prophet," yet others might not be happy with that name--Muslims and Jews perhaps because it means so much, Hindus and Buddhists because it means so little to them. There is one context where "prophet" may be used without hesitation: syncretistic set-ups where holy men and women wittingly imitate the *nabi* of the Hebrew Bible.

The appearance comes first, and the naming of the phenomenon follows. This is the sequence taught by van der Leeuw. But every so often it goes the other way round. Names are there and have been there centuries before phenomenology of religion was invented. Since then phenomenologists have tried to find some meat and bones which, calling those names, they could point to. Some seem to think the name is an essential component of that for which it stands. They explain it etymologically. One step further and the name becomes detached altogether from the thing it names. It then begins a life of its own as a concept inside some scholarly heads. Concepts appear in print on paper. Phenomena appear in a different manner.

Religious phenomena do not need a phenomenologist to come into existence. They are found wherever religion is to be found. But how do we study them best? For some time now there has been campaigning within Religionswissenschaft for what are called objective methods modeled after those of science. Scientific methods adequate for the religious realm boil down to comparison. Joachim Wach advertised the "objective study" of the many parts of which religions are made. He termed such studies Systematische Religionswissenschaft (Wach 1924) and divided them up into a basic part called "material" and a crowning part called "formal." According to him, we begin with material comparison, i.e., within a set area, defined by religious and geographical or temporal limits. To keep inside of one religion helps to avoid some pitfalls of the method. Material comparison has been tried by some. Bengt G. M. Sundkler, for example, compared prophets in South Africa and brought to light the twin categories of "Ethiopian" and "Zionist" (Sundkler 1948). I have, backed by Harold W. Turner's collection of source material, compared prophets in West Africa and come upon some constant links between their calls and their callings (Greschat 1974).

A chemical compound is composed alike in Asia and in Africa. Typhoid fever and diphtheria endanger the health of Christians no less than the health of Hindus. A flock of geese studied is taken to represent their entire species. But what do studies of prophets in Africa reveal of prophets in Asia and in America? We cannot say for sure, since we know how different faiths and different cultures tend to form religious items differently.

A universally valid prophet is an abstraction. The objective method producing abstractions within Religionswissenschaft is comparison. The method producing universal abstractions is universal comparison. Joachim Wach writes of "highest general concepts." Formal operations are to create such concepts, threshing so to speak what material operations have yet to gather in, comparing step by step all prophets of all religions. For highest general concepts complete world-sets of area studies are needed.

Here we get into trouble, for material comparisons of prophets are too few to objectively attempt formulation of the highest general concept of prophet. All we can do meanwhile is to get along subjectively.

Subjective methods can turn out to be shortcuts, ways leading around obstacles, paths we can follow on our own feet, without having to depend upon others for public works and transport. One such method is thinking, the skill in which universities specialize. Taking as a point of departure what we have learned of prophets so far, we could either put a computer on the track or try ourselves to think up theories in answer to why prophet movements come into existence. Theories are the stock in the trade of academic specialists. They are rational and enlightening, but they are not religious phenomena.

Our problem is how to arrive by way of subjective methods at a general level above, as it were, particular religions or particular movements. Theories are one--phenomena are another--possibility to get there. The classical phenomenology of religion appears to lose more and more supporters. The phenomenological method has, as far as I know, not yet been applied strictly to the study of religious phenomena. It might be worthwhile to give it a try.

A phenomenon can be composed out of parts, yet it always appears as a whole, as something complete which disappears if the whole is broken up into its components. To put it psychologically, a phenomenon is a Gestalt. A Gestalt or a phenomenon is a figure and a background. If we relate, for example, the figure of what Rudolf Otto termed divination to the background prophet, we create a meaning. The relation between figure and background changes with our changing interest. What has been figure may turn into background with a new figure in front. This dynamic way of perception is not only subjective; it is personal.

Knowledge can be passed from one person to another. Personal knowledge is my own, not borrowed, not hearsay, but experienced. If I decide to relate it to others, what will happen? Those with a similar experience understand straightway; no commentaries or explanations are needed; they know what I am talking about. Others have no personal knowledge of what I describe. They use it as a common, borrowed piece of information. Not everybody can have personally experienced a particular religious phenomenon. Yet some have, and they will understand forthwith.

Phenomenological descriptions thus exemplify items of Religionswissenschaft. With examples it is quality that counts, not quantity. The model case stands for the many individual cases. This does not make phenomenology the only method fit for the entire field of religion. Some problems find solution through questionnaires, some through textual criticism, and some through exemplification.

Phenomenology is said to work, but on condition only that we learn to ignore methodically the many and manifold thoughts, concepts, formulas, and theories generations of scholars have produced and sorted in the granaries of learning. We are to keep ourselves from taking a phenomenon apart, from analyzing it, subjecting it to tests, experimenting with it, defining it, explaining it etymologically, rethinking it into a concept or into a theory. In other words, phenomenologists are to imitate neither scientist nor scholar. Putting aside for the time being all they have ever heard or read or thought about a religious matter, they are to become aware of the phenomenon, of what appears.

REFERENCES

Greschat, Hans-Jürgen
  1974   *Westafrikanische Propheten*. Marburg.
Heiler, Friedrich
  1961   *Erscheinungsformen und Wesen der Religion*. Stuttgart:
          W. Kohlhammer. Die Religionen der Menschheit 1.
Otto, Rudolf
  1969   *The Idea of the Holy*. trans. by John W. Harvey, London:
          Oxford University Press.
Spence, Lewis
  1919   "Prophecy, American," *Encyclopaedia of Religion and
          Ethics*, Vol. X, ed. by James Hastings, New York:
          Charles Scribner's Sons.
Sundkler, Bengt G. M.
  1948   *Bantu Prophets in South Africa*. London: International
          African Institute.
Van der Leeuw, Gerardus
  1970   *Phänomenologie der Religion*. Tubingen: J. C. B. Mohr.
          Neue Theologische Grundrisse.
Wach, Joachim
  1924   *Prolegomena zu ihrer Wissenschaftstheorekischen
          Grundlegung*. Leipzig: J. C. Hinrichs.
Widengren, Geo.
  1969   *Religionsphänomenologie*. Berlin: de Gruyter Lehrbuch.

Hans-Jürgen Greschat

P. R. McKenzie
University of Leicester

Phenomenology and "the Centre" —the Leicester years

In 1966 Harold Turner began teaching Phenomenology and History of Religion in a one-year course at Leicester University with eight students. He also put forward at Leicester a plan for a Centre for New Religious Movements. This brief account based on records in the Department of Religion at Leicester is concerned with the way the teaching of phenomenology and the plan for a centre were received at the time.

Early in the following autumn, with one full session behind him, Harold Turner wrote to the Vice-Chancellor Mr. (later Sir) Fraser Noble with far-reaching proposals for further developments of the course in phenomenology. They were based on the principle earlier accepted by the university that the Leicester program should occupy a field not found or well-developed in other British universities, including those of neighboring Nottingham, Birmingham, or Warwick. Turner sketched the outline of a second and third year of the course in which prophetic religions would feature history of religion in the second year, Christianity and Islam being taken further in year three alongside Indian religion and "primal" religions of a particular area. One reason for this was the connection with the plan for a special centre for new religious movements.

The phenomenology courses in years two and three are not spelled out in the document, but from accompanying notes in the file we see that year two would include such topics as types of religions, religious persons and communities, symbolism, conversion, prayer, and eschatology. Year three's categories are sketched out as incarnation, salvation, sacrifice and sacraments, initiation, purification and "fertility" cosmologies. This three-year course would be cared for in a Department of Phenomenology and History of Religion. As if this plan were not sufficient for the university's Development Board to have to swallow, Harold Turner proceeded to add his plan for a post-graduate centre for primal religions and new movements. The department with its three-year course and the post-graduate centre were to be set up and staffed, in stages over a period of three years, with three lecturers for the former and a bibliographer and a research fellow for the latter.

We are not told of the Vice-Chancellor's immediate reaction, but that of a colleague who later became a Regius professor at Oxford has been preserved: "You'll meet," he predicted gloomily, "with a solid phalanx of opposition, for nothing seems to scare academics so much as the mention of 'religion.' " He added: "What you'll be doing is very much out of touch with the interests of most of our colleagues here and most of our teaching."

Early in 1968 came a more friendly, but also in its way discouraging, reply from the Vice-Chancellor reporting on the Development Board's discussion of the Turner memorandum. Financial reasons were given as the main hindrance to implementing the plan. He suggested meanwhile that the proposal should be the subject of continued informal discussions. Later in the year, however, we find further progress with phenomenology. Second-year regulations were approved by Senate. But the project for a centre was held up. By June it was apparent that the Development Board had firmly turned down the idea of a centre for primal religions and new movements. The reason given was the lack of cognate fields of study, especially anthropology. Victorian studies was cited as an instance of a centre which did have scholars from other departments cooperating. Despite its rejection of the plan for the centre, the board left the door open for a second lectureship in phenomenology. This would, however, take time in view of "the existing financial crisis."

In November 1969, Harold Turner approached his head of department and through this the Establishment Board, for a second lecturer. His case rested on the increasing numbers of the first year (now up to 28) which would soon exceed the capability of one lecturer to cope with effectively. There was also extensive post-graduate and B.Ed. work. The following month the Committee of Vice-

Chancellors and Principals provided unexpected support. They issued a document entitled *University Development in the 1970s* which spoke openly of further expansion on the basis of increasing numbers of school leavers. Hopes of an early decision to appoint a second lecturer could now be realized. Approval was given, and applications were called for in March 1970. By that time, however, Harold Turner had begun reluctantly to look elsewhere for the realization of the plan for the centre. It looked as if the Centre for New Religious Movements would be given a home at Lancaster University, since it was being made part of Lancaster's development plan for 1972-1977. Eventually it began at the University of Aberdeen; and at the time of writing, it has become established at the Selly Oak Colleges in Birmingham not far from Leicester.

But this is to anticipate. Having secured the second lecturer, Harold Turner then boldly resigned from Leicester to accept a temporary appointment as visiting professor in Atlanta, Georgia. There followed what today would surely have to be regarded as outside the realm of possibility. He was able to secure additional approval for a replacement for himself. This meant the realization of stage one of his 1967 three-stage plan: in October two lecturers, Dr. P. R. McKenzie and Mr. S. J. Reno, could begin the two-year program. Numbers continued to increase so that in 1972 a tutorial assistantship was approved and in 1974 (with 85 in the first-year class and 36 in the second) a third lectureship was agreed to. Mr. A. D. Brear was appointed each time. In October 1974 the third-year course in Phenomenology and History of Religion could be introduced, and in 1977 a Department of Religion was established. The department as envisaged by Harold Turner had now come into being to look after a three-year course featuring phenomenology and traditional or ethnic religions as well as Asian and prophetic religions. The 1974 three-year course was modified to take into account the interests of the lecturers concerned; and future years would see further modifications, especially the beginning of Asian religions and Christianity earlier in the course, and the introduction of Amerindian religions to strengthen further the ethnic religions component. Nevertheless, in its basic structure the 1974 three-year course represents Harold Turner's 1967 outline in its main structure, as may be seen in the following outline:

P. R. McKenzie

Harold Turner 1967
Paper
Year One:
1. Theoretical & historical introductions
2. Phenomenology
Year Two:
1. Phenomenology
2. History
Year Three:
1. Phenomenology
2. History A
3. History B

1974-75 Course
Paper
Year One:
1. Introduction to the Study of Religion and African Traditional Religion
2. Phenomenology (Myth, Sacred Action, Sacred Time, Sacred Space)
Year Two:
1. Phenomenology (Initiation, Holy Man & Deities, Sacred Worldview)
2. History (Zoroastrianism, Judaism, Islam)
Year Three:
1. Phenomenology (Sacred Symbols & Images, Sacred Community, Sacred Word & Silence, Sacred Writings)
2. History of Religion A (Christianity)
3. History of Religion B (Hinduism & Buddhism)

The Leicester three-year course in Phenomenology and History of Religion lasted just ten years, from its inception in 1974 to its last graduating class in 1984. Over that period it was ranked seventh in terms of popularity among the 16 subjects in Combined Arts. Yet the 1981 cuts fell harshly upon this course, reducing it to a one- and two-year service course, which is still in trouble with the fresh round of cuts (1985-1990). Despite sharing so fully in the troubles of small departments of religion however, it remains an example of a popular degree in religion with a coherent rationale, offering a nice blend of interdisciplinary work (combined with other subjects) and also providing a simple progression through three years of phenomenology paralleled by three years of complementary studies in the history of religion. Looking back to the Leicester years of Harold Turner, we may say that with respect to his twin projects--the degree in phenomenology and the Centre for New Religious Movements--the former only was realized at Leicester, and that four years after his timetable. The Centre, although turned down at Leicester, came into being at Aberdeen and Birmingham. Of the two projects, the Centre may be proving the more durable on the margins of the hard-pressed university system, not within it. It is intriguing to speculate whether, if the degree course and the Centre had been simultaneously implemented at Leicester, the presence of the post-graduate centre could have prevented the demise of the third year of the Honours course at the time of the cuts. Certainly there was strong resistance to the Centre at the time and, equally, a department of three lecturers was scarcely strong enough safely to weather the storms to come. Given the real university world, one must conclude that Turner's plans for Leicester during 1966-70 achieved a surprising degree of success.

One further reflection: The undergraduate course and the post-graduate centre were seen as complementing each other and do surely still need each other. Perhaps in future years there may be some way of establishing some kind of link between them.

P. R. McKenzie

James Thrower
University of Aberdeen

Harold Turner is a scholar who has ever sought to explore the religious possibilities inherent in any situation in which he found himself. His question to me (at that time a humanist), therefore, and which I here seek to answer, was:

Has humanism a religious dimension?

Humanist is one of those labels that almost all lay claim to and which few would deny as being applicable to their outlook on life, whether that outlook be overtly religious or outright atheistic. We thus hear much about Christian humanism, Marxist humanism, and existentialist humanism. Let me therefore say that the humanism that I shall be concerned with here is the humanism of those associations in Britain and elsewhere with which Harold Turner sought on occasions to make contact and which consciously use this term, and this term alone, to describe their outlook on life and their program for action.

While we must recognize--as Susan Budd, a student of contemporary humanism, has pointed out--that humanism has no single, clear-cut system, its adherents do have certain attitudes in common, not least with regard to religion (Budd 1967:377-465). Prima facie at least, the humanist associations with which I shall be concerned are characterized, perhaps above all else, by an overt rejection of any and every religious understanding of the world and of humans and their destiny--at least as this has been traditionally understood within the historic religions.

Thus the British Humanist Association states in one of its policy documents, *The Humanist Alternative*, that human problems must be faced in terms of man's intellectual and moral resources without invoking supernatural authority. It states elsewhere, in *Humanism and Humanists*, that "we cannot depend on any superhuman guide to tell us how we should live; the individual must therefore depend upon his own intellectual and moral resources and upon the help of other people. The humanist's concern is with life in this world. For practical purposes, the assumption is made that man is on his own and this life is all."

Similarly, *Humanist Manifesto II* (1973), a policy document circulated by the American and British Humanist Associations and signed by leading humanists in both countries as well as by the chairmen of the Indian, Dutch, and other national associations, states with regard to religion that the signatories believe that traditional dogmatic or authoritarian religions that place revelation, God, ritual, or creed above human needs and experience do a disservice to the human species. Any account of nature, the signatories continue, should pass the tests of scientific evidence; in our judgment, the dogmas and myths of traditional religion do not do so. . . . We find insufficient evidence for belief in the existence of a supernatural; it is either meaningless or irrelevant to the question of the survival and fulfilment of the human race. As non-theists, we begin with humans not God, nature not deity. Nature may indeed be broader and deeper than we now know; any new discoveries, however, will but enlarge our knowledge of the natural.

More significantly the document continues: "Some humanists believe we should reinterpret traditional religions and reinvest them with meanings appropriate to the current situation. Such redefinitions, however, often perpetrate old dependencies and escapisms; they easily become obscurantist, impeding the free use of the intellect. We need, instead, radically new human purposes and goals."

This last sentence is important, for there are within the humanist movements those who still wish to retain the language, if not the substance, of traditional religion. That this is not the position of the majority of the leaders of the international humanist movement will, I hope, be clear from the quotations given. The reasons for regarding the problems that face us as human beings as human problems that the signatories to *Humanist Manifesto II* give are worth noting, for they go some way to helping us understand why many humanists resent their outlook on life being designated "religious." They write:

> Traditional religions often offer solace to humans, but, as often, they inhibit humans from helping themselves or experiencing their full potentialities. Such institutions, creeds, and rituals often impede the will to serve others. Too often traditional faiths encourage dependence rather than independence, obedience rather than affirmation, fear rather than courage. ... Promises of eternal salvation or fear of eternal damnation are both illusory and harmful. They distract humans from present concerns, from self-actualisation, and from rectifying social injustices (*Humanist Manifesto II*, 1973).

Which of us with any acquaintance with the history of religions can deny that religion has at times--and in some cases all of the time--subserved this function? The examples are legion.

J. P. van Praag, the chairman of the International Humanist and Ethical Union, opened the second Catholic-Humanist Dialogue in Brussels in 1970 with a paper entitled "The Humanist Outlook" with a list of ten postulates which he took to be fundamental to all forms of secular humanism. Postulates 2, 8, and 9 read as follows:

> 2 Secularity. Men are part of, and disposed to, their world. Man springs from a reality of which he himself is a 'natural' part. As such he is a conjunction of relations. But he is also a centre of action. As an intentional being he shapes his world both mentally and in reality.
>
> 8 Completeness. The world is complete and does not imply an upper or outer world. Completeness is not perfection, but means that the world is not thought of as dependent on a creator, nor is there any empty place left vacant by an absent creator.
>
> 9 Contingency. The world does not reveal meaning, either as harmony or as direction. It is man who puts questions and contributes meaning. The world does not furnish a guarantee for human living, but rather a framework for human development (Kurtz and Dondeyne 1972:5-6).

But perhaps the most thorough statement of what is involved in humanism--in the sense in which I am using the term--is that put forward by Ronald Fletcher in a pamphlet issued by the Rationalist Press Association and sent to all new members upon payment of their first subscription. In this pamphlet, *A Definition of Humanism* (n.d.), Fletcher urges four principles as characteristic of humanism.

First, he says, humanism is human-centered in matters of knowledge and judgment. The only knowledge we can have is human knowledge, and all human knowledge is knowledge of the world as we, as human beings, experience it. We can never possibly accept doctrines which go beyond the range of human experience and the procedures of testability. Within a humanism so defined there can be no room for faith as this is understood by religious people; such faith could not be a criterion of truth for the simple reason that it is of equal validity for all religions. On such a criterion all religions would be equally true. This is manifestly absurd, says Fletcher, in that religions quite frequently contradict each other. The only sense in which a humanist could be said to have faith is where faith is understood as witnessing to the fact that when the boundaries of knowledge have been reached, humanists, like many others, feel that there is more to be explored, more than that which constitutes knowledge at any given point in history. Such feelings are, for the humanist, but an invitation to seek for further clarity and depth in our knowledge and have little or nothing to do with faith in any religious meaning of that term.

Second, humanism is human-concerned in that it exhibits a sensitive compassion for the well-being of all people as the basis of its morality. The humanist's concern, writes Fletcher, "is to achieve a kind of society in which all men can make their claims for the kinds and conditions of life which for them lead to happiness and fulfilment." Humanism, therefore, emphasizes freedom and tolerance.

Third, humanism is not, as some antagonists have maintained, human-confined, by which Fletcher means that humanism is not insensitive to the larger horizons and rich subtleties of the non-human world. Humanists, he maintains, can be as sensitive to the many-sided enigma of nature--to its beauties, sublimities, meannesses, cruelties, fatefulness, varieties of mood--as anyone else. "As far as I can see [he writes] he [the humanist] is as much a prey to all the feelings, 'intimations,' doubts, and baffling questions that confront us in trying to fathom the tangled skein of nature as anyone else." And he adds:

> A sensitive vulnerability to all the dimensions of our entanglement in the world, and the desire to probe and to articulate the experience of some deeply felt meaning in it all, are not exclusive to

religions. They are equally open to those of us who cannot easily find our way. . . . Such experience seems to me not a matter of mysticism at all . . . but a matter of sheer, conscious, everyday, inescapable fact: that our human nature is rooted in the nature of the world; that all the interwoven, patterned, marvellous, but often terrible, elements of the world of nature are in some way elements of our own physical, emotional, mental, and spiritual nature. . . . The one and the many is not a mystical insight, it is a common everyday truth.

Fourth and last, humanism insists that testable knowledge provides the only reliable basis for interpreting the world and for personal, social, and political action.

To these four cardinal principles Fletcher adds that humanists insist that self-responsibility is the only satisfactory and effective basis for individual development. Humanism is, therefore, anti-authoritarian and tolerant of others. Morality, for the humanist, is also quite independent of the certainty of any and all religious doctrines (Fletcher n.d.).

From the above statements, which are typical of what I would call "mainstream humanism," it would be difficult to ascribe to such humanism a religious dimension--at least in the sense in which this term is ordinarily understood. Such an ascription is both implicitly, and often explicitly, rejected. Ronald Fletcher, for instance, does indeed raise the question, "Is humanism a religion?" but answers it in the negative. He writes: "I personally, think one ought to say that it is not in the sense that it does not and cannot pretend to the kinds of ultimate doctrines or the supporting rituals which religious systems provide. Indeed it does not require them" (Fletcher n.d.:14).

Fletcher also recognizes that humanism cannot provide answers to many of the questions to which religion professes to provide answers--questions relating to ultimate meaning, to some final resolution of personal life which will be altogether satisfactory, questions relating to personal immortality. Humanism, he says, has to recognize also an inescapable undertone of tragedy in the world:

Ultimately, the situation of mankind in the world is a tragic one. Human life is transient. Nature is an enigma into which we can only see so far. No man can ever fathom it. Our human condition is one which must suffer ultimate loss. All that we are, all that we love, all those things, people, and values to which and to whom we are attached by love, perish. Nothing of individual nature seems permanent. Nothing is certain. Humanism can offer no consolation (Fletcher n.d.:13).

Van Praag goes further and holds that not only does humanism not provide final answers to fundamental questions but "puts different questions":

> The humanist is not a Christian stripped of his Christian expectations and attitudes; he has a different approach. . . . Humanism does not substitute another certainty for the certainty of the gospels, nor another security for the security in God, nor another ultimate goal for eternal salvation. It takes seriously the temporality of human life and does not assume that anything can overcome death. . . . It simply assumes the possibility of a significant life in trial and error, with no other guarantee than man's inextinguishable endeavour, and without any other worldly purpose. In the humanist conception life bears its ultimate goals in itself (Kurtz and Dondeyne 1972:7-8).

Harold Blackham, until recently the director of the British Humanist Association, made a similar point when he wrote in his second contribution to the symposium, *Objections to Humanism*:

> If one starts from the Christian point of view, humanism is merely an exercise in vital subtraction. . . . There is a type of humanist who is a Christian manqué . . . but he is not representative. Nor is the humanist a fox without a tail; if he has no tail, it is because he is a different breed of fox. He is not looking at the Christian world without faith and hope. He has turned completely round and sees another scene. He starts with a positive acceptance and appreciation of the conditions of the natural world, and gladly gathers the perishable happiness that is to be had and enjoyed (Blackham 1965:105).

Earlier, Blackham, like Fletcher, had raised the question whether humanism was a religion--only, like Fletcher, to dismiss it. Humanists, he wrote, "do not normally preserve age-old religious categories in their thinking (numinous, holy, sacred, absolute, transcendent, divine) and modernise their content" (Blackham 1965:24).

In the light of the clear rejection of any inherently religious dimension to humanism by what I take to be representative, authoritative spokesmen of contemporary humanism, it would be difficult to impute to humanism anything overtly religious. But, of course, the question can still be raised whether there is, perhaps, an *implicit* religious dimension to humanism. The question becomes more per-tinent when we note that despite what the authoritative representa-tive may say, many within certainly the British humanist movement have themselves claimed that humanism has such a dimension.

In 1975 Sir Richard Acland, himself a radical Christian on his own admission, appealed in the pages of the journal of the Rationalist Press Association, *New Humanist*, for an alliance of radi-cal Christians and what he identified as "religious Humanists," against the rigidly orthodox in both their persuasions. In his article Acland identified two wings within the current humanist movement: the orthodox, among whom he numbered A. J. Ayer, Peter Medawar, and the French scientist Jacques Monod; and the religious, represented by such noted figures as Julian Huxley and the now president of the British Humanist Association, James Hemming. These latter were described as religious by Acland almost solely on the grounds that they accepted that we live in a mysterious universe. He wrote:

> But there are . . . humanists whom I dare to describe as 'religious humanists.' By this I do not suggest that they perform any inner operation that could be described as 'believing in the existence of God.' I simply mean that, in words attributed to Aneurin Bevan by Jennie Lee, they know that 'at the heart of life there is a mystery.' Or, in the words of James Hemming in *Individual Morality* (1969), they accept themselves as being 'in a state of struggle, and of search, and of being, within a mystery.' Most of these humanists, I believe, would agree that in some strange way the whole of life on earth is bound together into an organic unity (Acland 1975:61).

The problem here is that most humanists would admit to living in a mysterious universe without in any sense seeing anything at all religious in such an admission. If this is all that there is to religious humanism, then it would be hard to avoid the conclusion that the dispute was but over a word. The late Margaret Knight commented in a reply to Acland, but with reference to some remarks of Peter Cadogan, the general secretary of The South Place Ethical Society, a body affiliated to the British Humanist Association, to the effect that the human being is a religious animal (in that) he is concerned with mystery, wonder, awe, imagination, enquiry, caring relationships, loyalty and the related needs of belonging and solitariness: If this is all that is implied by the term 'religious' it would seem that with negligible exceptions we are all religious humanists and the prefix is therefore superfluous (Knight 1975:68).

To support the case that she was eventually to make--that the differences between humanists are primarily temperamental--Knight conducted her own survey of the writing of those who describe themselves as religious humanists to endeavor to ascertain just what they understood by this description. She distinguished two different but related meanings of the term.

In the first meaning a religious humanist can be said to be one who holds humanist beliefs with the same dedication and fervor as is felt by the committed Christian, for instance. John Lewis, writing in *The Ethical Record*, the journal of the South Place Ethical Society, about the history of that institution and of the Bayswater Ethical Church noted that both bodies "always associated with their belief in reason and right an attitude of dedication and commitment that to the founders of both institutions represented a religious attitude" (Lewis 1974).

The second and more important meaning that Knight found was one in which a religious humanist is someone who believes that the good life involves something more than material prosperity. Failing to see anything particularly religious in either of these meanings she concluded--I think myself rightly--that the differences that exist between those who wish to describe themselves as religious humanists and those who do not is largely one of temperament. She writes:

> The difference between the extremes of the spectrum is not ... primarily a difference in strength of commitment to humanism, or in esteem for non-material values: it is basically just a difference of temperament, and can be crudely expressed by saying that secular humanists have a predominantly intellectual, and religious Humanists a predominantly emotional, approach to life. The difference between them comes out clearly in their use of language. Secular humanists set store by lucidity and precision; religious humanists tend to favor an "inspirational" vagueness with plenty of abstract nouns (Knight 1975:69).

This is illustrated, I think, by Peter Cadogan's reply to Knight's remarks in *The Ethical Record*. He wrote that Knight's point was "interesting" but "not good enough":

> It assumes a necessary conflict between the intellectual and the emotional with the one "predominating" over the other. But life is not like that. . . . Religion is a combination of beliefs and rituals concerned with the sacred as distinct from the profane. The sacred has no necessary connection with the supernatural or any revealed personal deity. The sacred is that which we set apart, revere, have faith in.

And in answer to the question, "What then is sacred for us?," Cadogan replied:

> "We believe: in caring and caring relationships; in the importance of people against things, possessions, power; in imaginative vision; in reasonable enquiry and plain speaking; in unity with nature; in belonging and solitariness; in civil and religious liberty; and that these being sacred, give meaning to life" (Cadogan 1975:68).

This, far from constituting a rejection of Knight's point, is, in fact, a perfect illustration of it. Only on the most vacuous definition of religion could the list which Cadogan gives of those things which for him are sacred could the sacred so described be considered in any sense religious. Certainly, historically and phenomenologically considered, the sacred, the religious, has had more substantive connotation than Cadogan and those who speak like him would seem to realize. For this reason most humanists quite categorically reject that term as in any way applicable to the beliefs that they hold. To this point I shall return shortly.

Sir Richard Acland, however, in the article to which we have referred, had in his description of religious humanism gone further than this:

> I believe that these religious humanists would also accept the proposition that in some way or other, out of the depths, there comes to each one of us an invitation or a purpose, even though the nature of the purpose can only be dimly foreseen. . . . Differing from radical Christians who would say that the call comes from God, the "religious" humanists would feel it as coming to their conscious minds from the depths of their own humanity or perhaps mysteriously from humanity as a whole (Acland 1975:6).

Here we reach the borderline between secular humanism and religious humanism, although I can think of interpretations of what I take Acland to be saying that need not necessarily be religious. The call to humans to be true to their nature, to fulfill themselves as humans, can be made by those with a secular vision of humans and their destiny as well as by those with a more traditionally religious vision. Everything here depends on one's conception of humans. Where, however, the conception of a purpose is thought of as coming not simply from what the nineteenth-century German philosophical tradition tended to refer to as humans' species nature but from a source without; where, for instance, the ongoing processes of nature are thought of as being under the providential guidance of some Cosmic Mind, where the Universe is thought of as in some sense "on our side"--to draw on the language of the kind of humanism I have in mind--then, I think, we can speak sensibly of a truly religious dimension to such humanism.

My impression is, however, that on the whole, such people tend to break with what I would regard as mainstream humanism and to found separate, explicitly Religious Humanist Associations, often in close alliance with like-minded religious sects such as the Unitarians and the Quakers. It must be recognized, however, that certainly in Britain such religious humanists still haunt the fringes of the humanist movement. In view of this it would be correct, therefore, to speak of a religious dimension to humanism, but I take it that the question once posed to me by Harold Turner was asking about a possible religious dimension to humanism in some sense other than this rather obvious one. The question as I understand it relates to the possibility that, despite the overt denials of many of the representative spokespersons of contemporary humanism, there is in humanism a covert, implicit religious dimension.

As will be obvious, much, if not everything, here depends on how we are to understand the term "religious," and our task is not made any the easier by the fact, as we have seen, that humanists themselves are not agreed upon its meaning and so upon its applicability or otherwise to themselves. The situation is further complicated, of course, by the fact that in Western Europe and America traditional religion--by which I mean the Christian religion--is also changing.

In such a fluid situation it has been suggested that we get little from substantive definitions of religion. As J. Milton Yinger has remarked in *The Scientific Study of Religion*:

> Substantive definitions can be of great value, particularly for those who are concerned with religions as historical and cultural facts rather than with religion as a panhuman phenomenon. They are of greater value in the study of stable societies, where distinctive and coherent religious systems are likely to develop, than they are in the study of changing societies; for in the latter, religion itself is also in the process of changing, which continually complicates any attempt to define what it is, but equally suggests new efforts to study what it does (Yinger 1970:4).

This does not negate the fact, however, that the term "religion" comes to us, within the tradition which we inherit, with certain historical connotations--however fluid that tradition may now have become--and that because of this, many humanists are led to reject the term as being applicable to their beliefs. It is not just that such historical connotations lag behind those of the more theologically advanced, but that large numbers of people, and not all of them at all theologically immature, reject the new connotations as a detraction from, rather than as an advance upon, what has gone before. The interesting thing is that many humanists agree with them! Thus Knight could write:

> But this is not quite all that needs to be said, for an alliance of the type [Acland] proposed would require far greater concessions on the humanist side than just endorsing Acland's nebulous views about the Logos. It would imply our giving our approval, explicitly or implicitly, to the whole farrago of sloppy thinking and intellectual shiftiness that makes up current liberal theology (Knight 1975:69).

We must thus recognize that there is a fairly broad spectrum within religion also, one end of which shades just as imperceptibly into humanism as does humanism into religion. As Alasdair MacIntyre wrote of John Robinson's book, *Honest to God*, there is little in its view of the world which a sophisticated and refined humanism could not incorporate into itself (Robinson and Edwards n.d.:34). The days of crude mechanicomaterialism are as dead to the humanist as they are to others.

This grey area between religion and humanism I shall leave as so much disputed territory and conclude that on a substantial definition of religion it would be hard, if not impossible, to maintain that there is a religious dimension to humanism.

James Thrower

If, on the other hand, we employ a functional definition and define religion and humanism in terms of the functions which they fulfill, the role which they play, then more positive conclusions emerge with regard to the possible religious dimensions of humanism. In that they are both life-orientations, religion and humanism would appear, prima facie, to subserve similar needs both of the individual and, if not today of society as a whole, of sub-cultures within society. On such a definition the truly irreligious individual, the truly irreligious society, would be one in which there was no such overall life-orientation. As Helmut Thielike noted vis 'a vis such individuals, they do not ask ultimate questions. In fact, as he says, these questions are on the whole asked only by those who still stand in some sort of relationship with the Christian church--a point to which I shall return at the close of this paper.

The religious person, on the other hand, is one who is concerned with ultimate questions as, to quote the list given by Milton Yinger in his study of functional definitions of religion:

> How shall we respond to the fact of death? Does life have some central meaning despite the suffering and the succession of frustrations and tragedies it brings with it? How can we deal with the forces that press in upon us, endangering our livelihood, our health, and the survival and smooth operation of the groups in which we live--forces that our empirical knowledge cannot handle adequately? How can we bring our capacity for hostility and our egocentricity sufficiently under control to allow the groups within which we live . . . to be kept together? (Yinger 1970).

If these are--as Yinger claims--the religious questions and insofar as humanism certainly offers answers to them, then there is obviously a religious dimension to humanism.

But are they religious questions? Certainly in the past, religion has provided the framework within which these and like questions have been both raised and answered. But today, it seems to me, it makes just as much sense to regard these questions as human questions as it does to regard them as religious. As Yinger himself writes:

> These questions appear to be both rational and self-conscious. They are more appropriately seen, however, as deep-seated emotional needs, springing from the very nature of man as an individual and as a member of society. The questions appear first of all because

they are felt. ... Religion may develop an intellectual system to interpret and deal with these questions, but they must be seen first of all not as a group of rationally conceived problems, but as expressions of an underlying emotional need (Yinger 1970:6-7).

Further, religious rituals can be seen, as is argued by the Oxford anthropologist John Beattie, as expressive attempts to do something about these "limit" situations of human existence. This, for Beattie, is of the essence of religion--primitive and developed. He writes:

Basically, [religion] expresses [man's] fundamental dependence on the natural world which he occupies and of which he is part. We have seen that much ritual and religious behaviour translates uncontrollable natural forces into symbolic entities which, through the performance of ritual, can be manipulated and dealt with. Ritual is a language for saying things which are felt to be true and important but which are not susceptible of statement in scientific terms. ... And in the areas beyond science there is no way of expressing it except symbolically (Beattie 1966:239).

Insofar as humanism has sought to offer substitute ceremonies to religious ceremonies--particularly in the area that anthropologists refer to as rites of passage--then we have a further example of humanism seeking to take over at least some of the traditional functions of religion. But, again, it would make just as much sense to speak of these as essentially human ceremonies, as attempts to come to a human resolution of the emotional tension that these situations arouse.

In that religious people, perhaps from a psychological point of view simply as people, seek for a similar resolution of their emotions in certain situations, and because in the past such was the dominant way, we are tempted to regard any and every attempt at such a resolution as religious. My point is quite simply that this need not be so. It is possible, and for the humanist essential, to regard these problems--emotionally and intellectually--as human problems and to seek for purely human solutions. If Blackham's "Man is on his own; this world is all" is of the essence of humanism, then, in the light of religion's truck with the transcendent, to describe such problems and their resolution as religious, however different religion and humanism's respective resolutions might be, is simply to blur issues which humanists, and indeed many religious people, see as supremely important.

The important question is not one concerning the functions which religion and humanism fulfill but one concerning the concrete solutions which they propose. Of course it is possible to define religion-- functionally and even substantially--so that all and every philosophy of life is subsumed under the definition. But the question remains, "To what point? What is gained by such a definition?" In that issues have been blurred, it could be maintained, that much has been lost. A blanket definition of religion in which none, or at least few, can be said to be non-religious may give comfort to those religious people who wish to feel that all are for them and none against them, but one cannot surely sweep away the real differences that exist between humanists and the religious of the world simply by means of a redefinition of religion.

Bertrand Russell once remarked, in a biting criticism of linguistic philosophy, that a clergyman who lost his faith abandoned his orders; a philosopher simply redefined his subject. My feeling today is that the clergy are learning from the philosophers. But just as the perennial problems of philosophy did not go away simply because certain philosophers did not know how to answer them, so the essential differences between religious--in the sense in which this word is commonly used to designate certain specific, concrete beliefs and activities in the cultures of the world--and humanist outlooks on the world remain. Humanism, I as a humanist would maintain, has not got a religious dimension in anything other than the sense which would see all attempts to handle the fundamental questions of the human condition as religious. While this may be expressive of a belief in our common humanity, it does not get us far towards solving the problems that bedevil us.

There is one vantage point, however, from which it makes sense to speak of a religious dimension to present-day humanism, of mainstream humanism, that is. Opposites, as Aristotle maintained, belong to the same genus and insofar as humanism, historically and still, to a large extent, to the present day, founds itself upon its rejection of religion, it is open to the charge that it has not passed beyond the sphere of the religious--a charge that Karl Marx brought against the humanism of Feuerbach and the "left" Hegelians of his own day. As he wrote in the *Economic and Philosophic Manuscripts of 1844*:

> The question of an alien being about a being above nature and man--a question which implies the admission of the inessentiality of nature and man--has become virtually impossible. Atheism, as the disavowal of this inessentiality, has no longer any meaning, for atheism is a negation of God and postulates the existence of man through this negation; but socialism qua socialism no longer stands in need of such a mediation (Marx and Engels 1975:305-06).

Much contemporary humanism thrives on anti-religious polemic; no one who is familiar with its literature will deny that. Insofar as this constitutes its raison d'être it is still, in my opinion, confined within a "form of life"--to use Wittgenstein's phrase--which is essentially religious. The truly secular person does not pay religion the compliment of refutation. But, with Harold Turner, I would today be more inclined to the opinion that there cannot be such a person.

REFERENCES
Acland, Richard
    1975   "Religious Humanism," *New Humanist*, 91(1) May.
Beattie, John
    1966   *Other Cultures*. London.
Blackham, H. J., ed.
    1965   *Objections to Humanism*. London.
British Humanist Association
    1973   *Humanist Manifesto II*. London.
Budd, Susan
    1967   "The Humanist Societies," *Patterns of Sectarianism*, ed. by Bryan Wilson. London.
Cadogan, Peter
    1975   Quoted in Margaret Knight, "Religious Humanism?" *New Humanist*, 91:3, July.
Fletcher, Ronald
    n.d.   *A Definition of Humanism*. London: Rationalist Press Association.
Knight, Margaret
    1975   "Religious Humanism?" *New Humanist*, 91:3, July.

James Thrower

Kurtz, Paul, and Albert Dondeyne, eds.
   1972   *A Catholic/Humanist Dialogue*. London.
Lewis, John
   1974   In *The Ethical Record*, February.
Marx, Karl, and Friedrich Engels
   1975-   *Collected Works*, Vol. 3, London.
Robinson, John, and David Edwards, eds.
   n.d.   *The Honest to God Debate*. London.
Thielike, Helmut
   n.d.   "Der Mensch des Sakularismus," *Universitas*, I:9, II:1.
Yinger, J. Milton
   1970   *The Scientific Study of Religion*. London.

James Irwin
Whakatane, New Zealand

Maori primal religion

The first European contact with the New Zealand Maori people began in the late eighteenth century. Explorers, whalers, traders, runaway sailors, and convicts were small in number but had a modifying effect upon both the culture and the environment. They introduced new technology with their iron and steel tools and weapons, new foods, new customs, and intoxicating liquor, and they had a healthy appetite for timber and flax. In many of these contacts the newcomers were welcomed and married Maori women. Some intrepid young Maori men began to make voyages to Australia as sailors on trading vessels, and they returned home with stories of new wonders. Thus when the first Church Missionary Society agents arrived in 1814, the Maori people in various parts of the country had begun to feel the effects of these non-Maori contacts; so the process of culture change had already begun by the time Samuel Marsden preached the first Christmas sermon at Oihi, Bay of Islands, December 25, 1814. Max Warren said of such missionaries:

> They were inner directed men who got their education the hard way who were prepared, believing they were led by the Holy Spirit, to follow a course of action which to others might seem inopportune, dangerous, or even subversive. . . . These men, coming from humble backgrounds, expected that the indigenous people converted to Christianity would also rise to the same responsibilities (*Social History* 36-57).

These expectations were shared by many of the early settlers of New Zealand. When, in 1859, the superintendent of the Province of Otago was asked to become the first president of a "Society for

James Irwin

Elevating the Conditions of the Maories" he agreed, setting down certain conditions. "He believed that if the Maoris were sober and industrious ... they could prosper in the same way as had the European settler" (Brooking 1984:123).

The impact of the missionaries was also affected by the methods they adopted to spread the Christian message.

> They came, expecting that the methods of evangelism tried and tested in England would work. They did not. They thought that on the model of Robinson Crusoe, a home and garden could be conjured out of the wilderness and Man Friday would emulate. He seldom did. They thought they could set a model of a Christian family and the Maori would follow. It rarely happened (Owens 1980:34).

Not all the early Christian missionaries were so cavalier. Thomas Kendall as early as 1815 published the first attempted handbook of the Maori language after only one year's residence. In 1824 he wrote describing his findings concerning the indigenous Maori religion; while these findings owe a great deal to Kendall's fertile interpretation, nevertheless he took seriously the idea of a valid Maori religious understanding of the universe (Binney 1968:171-76). Sadly, few of the missionaries were prepared to be as open as Kendall and generally dismissed such descriptions as superstitious rubbish. The French Catholic priest, Fr. C. Servant, was in New Zealand from 1838 to 1842 and quickly gained a good working knowledge of the Maori language. He described the life, customs, and beliefs of the people based on observation and Maori informants and was remarkably free from prejudice. However, in describing religious beliefs he wrote, "Nothing is more ridiculous than this credulity of theirs." "The means they use to protect themselves against the anger of the gods are the observance of tapous and the practice of a few superstitious ceremonies" (Servant 1973:50). I remember Harold Turner remarking during a lecture that "superstition is the left-over detritus of a forgotten religion." In the case of Maori religion, it was not forgotten but indeed part of the warp and woof of the life of the people.

It was inevitable that the first presenters of the Christian story who preached to the Maori people clothed their message in Western clothes. Even when proficient in the Maori language they continued simply translating into Maori their European theological concerns,

52

causing much confusion to the Maori mind and offering inadequate means of coping with the concerns of pre-European Maori religion (Owens 1980:35). The oversimplified belief that all that was required of a missionary was to learn the language and preach the good tidings was an inadequate base on which to build an indigenous Maori Christian Church. What was preached from the European understanding of Christian values was interpreted by the hearers in terms of their own worldview as expressed in their religious beliefs and practices. These are not enshrined in creedal statements but in myths, legends, and sagas, and expressed in the rituals of meeting, of death, of birth, and so on. A simple example of this is the ritual greetings of the *hongi*; where two people press noses together when greeting each other. It is a ritual that is deeply religious; in the act the two come into the closest connection where they in fact share their *bau ora* (breath of life). This refers to the Maori creation story where in the creation of woman the great Tane breathed into her the breath of life. Thus in religious terms the ritual is the celebration of life and is also a ritual means of reconciliation for two who may be estranged from each other. So the ritual is an expression of spirituality that reaches into the social structure of the people.

The Maori worldview

Thanks to the habit among nineteenth-century people of keeping personal journals, the requirements of missionary societies that agents submit regular reports, and the propensity of Europeans visiting New Zealand to publish accounts of their travels, a great deal of material has proven--when sifted--a valuable source of accounts of the myths and customs of the Maori people. By the mid-1840s the more academically inclined of the new settlers began to gather accounts of the myths from Maori informants. These were of varied value, for some collectors edited their gathered material so that texts from that period required careful scrutiny. But gradually it became clear that there was a genuine indigenous Maori religion, and that in some respects it seemed more developed than many of the South Pacific Islands religions. While this was of interest to some serious scholars, it was generally ignored and given little credence that there was a genuine Maori religion.

James Irwin

In 1860 a Maori senior elder gathered representatives of the leading *tohunga* (experts) from various tribes to persuade them to write down their knowledge of the religious understanding of life. The experts resisted at first until they realized that already the changes in Maori society were so far-reaching that their religious heritage was also endangered. It was first revealed at that gathering that there was a High God known only to specially trained initiates. According to the scribe, the priests were bound, by pain of death, never to reveal his name and always to conduct the *karakia* (prayers) appropriate to him in secluded places. His name was given as Io, with sixteen titles to describe his nature. This information was widely denied by even sympathetic observers who pointed out that the descriptions of Io given by Maori informants were close indeed to the Old Testament descriptions of the Jewish Supreme Being, Yahweh. Classically it was normal to ascribe twelve names to Io; however, there were sixteen names--in fact, one list gives eighteen and another fourteen, the latter as follows:

Io - the core of all gods; none excel him

Io-nui - he is greater than all other gods

Io-roa - his life is everlasting; he knows not death

Io-matua - he is the parent of all things

Io-matuakore - the parentless; he is nothing but himself

Io-taketake - permanent, all-enduring, complete, immovable

Io-te-pukenga - the source of all thought; nothing is outside his jurisdiction

Io-te-wananga - the source of all knowledge, whether good or evil

Io-te-toi-o-nga rangi - the crown of the heavens; none higher than the all knowing

Io-matanui - the all knowing

Io-mata-ngaro - the hidden (unseen) face unless he wishes

Io-mata-aho - is seen only as radiant light

Io-te-whiwhia - nothing exists except by the volition of Io

Io-uru-taku - the one who is totally sacred

These names, it was claimed, are clearly the result of post-Christian contact and owe more to the Old Testament than to pre-European Maori conceptions. It is worth noting that no images of this being were ever made; no sacrifices were made to him. The name Io as that of a god was certainly known in many Polynesian communities before the advent of the European (Irwin 1984:33-35). It is likely that the advent of Christianity influenced the language used in describing Io.

Ordinary people were not permitted to have any knowledge of Io--only the upper echelons of the priestly experts were trained as his devotees. It is interesting that in the myth of the creation of woman the search for the female element involved the departmental god Tane in a journey to the *Toi o nga rangi* (the highest of the twelve heavens) to secure the information from Io. That myth is certainly pre-European.

From the group of myths known as the Creation stories, we have a coherent account of the worldview of the Maori. The first story in the myth cycle relates how the primeval parents who remained ever in locked embrace were forced apart by their progeny who longed to escape from the moist darkness where they were pressed between their parents. By discussion, argument, disagreement, and finally consensus the parents were separated, Rangi becoming the Sky Father (the heavens above) while the Earth Mother, Papatuanuku, became Planet Earth. The freed sons struggled for supremacy over each other. One remained with Rangi and is designated Tawhirimatea (god of wind and hurricane), and he attacked his brothers to avenge their forcing the parents apart. One brother, Tangaroa, sought refuge in the sea and became the god of the seas; the brothers Rongo and Haumia took refuge in the earth and so became the god of agriculture and the god of uncultivated foods. Tane, who had led the revolt against his parents, took refuge from his vengeful brother and became the god of forests and birds and progenitor of the human race. Another of the brothers refused to hide from Tawhirimatea and gave battle and compelled him to retire from the contest. This being, Tumateuenga, thus became the war god invoked by war parties. One other brother who had become increasingly jealous of his siblings could not bear the light of the world and fled to the underworld where he presides over darkness and is considered the originator of all that is evil, including disease. He is said to have committed adultery by stealing one of the brothers' wives.

In all, Ranginui and Papatuanuku are said to have produced seventy sons, each of whom is named in the myths and has his place in the cosmogony of the Maori people. Those who have been named above were termed departmental gods by Elsdon Best who undertook exhaustive research into Maori mythology from the turn of this century and whose papers have now been published in full. Two volumes give exhaustive information culled from informants of various tribes on the religious beliefs of the people. However, while his information is of first importance, his interpretations must be taken with caution, for he reflects the early anthropological misunderstandings of his day (Best vols. 1, 2).

From the Creation myths it is clear that the Maori people held a three-tiered worldview:

1. The heavens (twelve in all) are realms of Ultimate Reality.
2. The earth is the realm of the human.
3. The underworld is the realm of the dead.

For Maori people life was a whole as the universe was a whole, and so there was no compartmentalization into secular and sacred. Each of the three realms of the universe interpenetrated each other, and this understanding of a holistic worldview dictated the means used to approach the sacred.

Maori religion did not have set times of formal religious observances such as are seen in the great world religions. Instead, appropriate rituals were carried out as the occasion required. For a minor matter a murmured phrase or incantation by the individual would be sufficient; for more serious matters a priestly expert would be called, as when a fishing expedition was setting out; this person, a specialist in addressing Tangaroa (the god of the seas and fishes), would chant the necessary incantations to protect the fishers and to ensure a fruitful venture. Such rituals were attended only by those who were participating in the venture. When the bird-snaring season or the *kumara* (sweet potato) planting time commenced, more elaborate and more public ceremonies were observed. When a serious illness occurred, a priest healer was sought out; his rituals could involve all members of the extended family who came together as the cause of the sickness was diagnosed, the necessary treatment decided upon, and then the rituals were carried out.

The rituals of death and other public occasions were extremely elaborate, extending over several days and involving the whole subtribe or even the full tribe. These ceremonies were observed on the *marae* (sacred forecourt) in front of the carved ancestral meeting house. The whole occasion was highly structured to ensure that all ritual requirements were fulfilled so that the deceased person would be fully inducted among the ancestors. The ceremonies began with the assembly of the local people at the *marae*; when the parties of visitors arrived to share in the funerary rites they were called to the *marae*. The first act was an ancient *karanga* (call) to the ancestors to come from the "shades" and be present. Then after a period of formalized weeping, elaborate speeches were made; all followed a definite protocol that was carefully adhered to. When the local orators concluded, the visitors replied again following the local *kawa* (protocol). First the ground was addressed as Papatuanuku (earth mother), thus acknowledging the link with creation; next the meeting house was addressed, for it represented the progenitors of the sub-tribe. Genealogies were recited, establishing links between the living and the dead. Then the speaker addressed the deceased person (this not only extolled the person but also was a formal means of reconciliation if that were required). The deceased was bade farewell to go on the journey to the ancient homeland and join the ancestors. This rite served two purposes, for it acknowledged the spiritual nature of the universe and enabled full and frank expressions of grief. Then the speech addressed the local chiefs and established the nature of the relationship of the speaker with both the deceased and the local sub-tribe. As he came to the conclusion of the speech, the orator would intone the words, *"He wau kua heke te tapu"* (a song to lift the tapu), and his supporters would join him in an ancient chant or one especially composed for the occasion. Then the visitors would rise and move forward to shake hands and *hongi* with each of the home folks in turn. Thus the highly ritualized proceedings enabled the personalizing of the expressions of grief. Following this the visitors would be summoned to a meal which was the final act of the rituals of encounter, for food was a significant factor in nullifying any malign influences which many have pertained to the visitors.

Behind all such rites was a structure that explained humankind's place in the universe and humans' spiritual nature and interrelationships with the world of the spirit and the mundane world. This structure is summed up in six words, each of which indicates a principle of understanding the relationships between the spiritual universe and Maori society.

Mauri is the "life principle" that is given to the newborn infant as it takes its first breath. This is termed the *hau ora* (living breath) and must be guarded carefully, lest it be destroyed or lost and the person perish. The *mauri* is that which makes an individual a person.

Mana is that gift from the spiritual world which gives a person self-hood and self-understanding. It is a complex term referring to the response of a particular god to the invocation offered by the priestly expert or the father shortly after the birth of the child.

Mana also refers to a person's status and prestige in the society. It is understood to be lodged in the person's *mauri*, and should that be violated then the *mana* will be lost and the individual ceases to be a real person. To be *mana-kore* indicates that the individual is literally worthless, as are slaves who have no *mana*.

Tapu is the word to indicate a complex system of prohibitions which have a strongly protective function which guards the individual's *mana*. These prohibitions must be scrupulously observed, for whether by deliberate intention or inadvertence they are breached, a person's *mana* (which is considered to be a power) ceases to be controlled and can harm the offender or the community to which he or she belongs.

Noa describes the status of any person to whom no *tapu* pertains. By the addition of the causative prefix *whaka* the compound *whakanoa* is made. This describes the rituals of purification that enable someone to be cleansed from the consequences of a breached *tapu* and to be restored to the ordinary community.

This group of words has both spiritual and social connotations for life as a whole. So do the final two words, although they are perhaps not so clearly apprehended.

Utu is commonly translated as "vengeance," but this is misleading. The word is far better understood as a process of equalization that maintains the balance and harmony of society and the spiritual and mundane worlds.

This principle extends across the whole of Maori life. Should a person be slain by another, *utu* is called for to equalize the situation, for not only has a life been lost but the stability of the society is threatened and the harmony of life disturbed. Yet the simple act of receiving a gift of food from a neighbor also calls for *utu* by, at some time in an appropriate situation, making a return gift. It is part of the ethic of people. Interestingly, in replying to a speech or a question one is said to *Whakautu*; by replying the balance is maintained.

Muru refers to a ritual that is designed to restore badly damaged relationships, especially those involving two sub-tribes, where, for example, there has been a grievous offense (such as stealing another man's wife). In the passive voice *murua* it is used to refer to the custom when an extended family (sub-tribe) offers to another family prized family heirlooms in seeking to wipe out an offense against that other family. When these are accepted and the offender is perhaps given a beating by the aggrieved party, then normal relations can be resumed. It is usual to hear this referred to as "plunder," but is properly referred to as "requital" or "forgiveness." This was understood by the early Christian translators when they rendered "forgive us our trespasses" as *"murua o matou hara."*

Conclusion

This brief outline of some features of primal Maori religion indicate that the Maori people had developed a worldview that kept them in harmony with a spiritual universe and enabled them to respond in meaningful ways. The values thus expressed have been in many cases Christianized and constantly appear in the modern rituals of meeting, in death experiences, and in their interaction with European New Zealanders. Too often these values are unrecognized by Europeans who are prone to dismiss Maori rituals as of no value in the modern world. Yet these values are essential to Maori self-identity, and to participate in Maori expressions of spirituality leads to mutual understanding and acceptance, each thereby enriching the other.

The contribution of Harold Turner to this process has been most profound on a far wider screen than of only the Maori situation. His research in African and North American Indian spirituality and his rigorously disciplined expression in lecture rooms and published works have significantly reoriented the thinking of many missionaries so that their work is more soundly based on developing strong

Christian values without repudiating the realities within their old belief systems.

As a philosopher, teacher, colleague, and friend, Harold Turner has strengthened the endeavors of those of us privileged to study under him. In the classroom he moved at a fast pace, but he always carried us with him. The clarity of his thought and the preciseness of his expression required little elucidation, although he always listened with care to any comment we had to offer. I count myself fortunate to have profited in learning from him.

GLOSSARY

karanga	to call
karakia	incantation, prayer
kawa	protocol
kumara	sweet potato
mana	supernatural power, status, prestige
mana kore	powerless, without mana
marae	forecourt of land where meeting house stands
mauri	life principle
muru	wipe out
murua	plunder, forgive
noa	common, ordinary, free from tapu
tapu	prohibition, sacred, set apart
tohunga	an expert in any skill
utu	satisfaction, return for anything, price
whakanoa	to make clean, removal of a tapu
whakautu	to make a settlement, reply

REFERENCES

Best, E.
   1924   *Maori Religion and Mythology, Part 1*. Wellington, New Zealand: Government Printer.
   1982   *Maori Religion and Mythology, Part 2*. Wellington, New Zealand: Government Printer.
Binney, J.
   1968   *The Legacy of Guilt*. Christchurch, New Zealand: Oxford University Press.

Brooking, T.
1984   *And Captain of Their Souls*. Dunedin, New Zealand:
        Otago Heritage Books.
Irwin, J.
1984   *An Introduction to Maori Religion*. Adelaide, Australia:
        Australian Association for the Study of Religions.
Owens, J.
1980   "The Unexpected Impact," *Religion in New Zealand*, ed.
        by C. Nichol and J. Veitch. Wellington, New Zealand:
        Religious Studies Department.
Servant, C.
1973   *Customs and Habits of New Zealanders, 1938-42*.
        Wellington, New Zealand: A. H. and A. W. Reed.

James Irwin

Lamin Sanneh
Yale University

New and old in Africa's religious heritage: Islam, Christianity and the African encounter

Both Christianity and Islam are a thousand years old in some places in Africa, and where they are of less antiquity they are no less distinguished by the depth and range of their appeal. The depth of historical penetration has combined with the extent of indigenous assimilation to establish the two religions as permanent features of the African religious landscape.

It is customary to deal with the issue of Christianity and Muslim expansion in Africa in terms of how successful *they* were in winning converts, a view of religious change which belittles the immense contribution of Africa to the process. Instead we should approach the matter by asking how successful Africa was in assimilating the two religions, understanding Africa in that formulation to mean its diverse religious traditions and practices. This second way of looking at the subject assumes the enduring vitality of African materials under the Christian or Islamic garb. It is essential, therefore, to sketch in aspects of the African background on the basis of which the new gods of the two religions were successfully domesticated.

The African paradigm

It would be misleading to pretend that Africa is a unity of form and spirit. On the contrary, nowhere is its diversity and complexity more evident than in the religious sphere. Yet the continent shares this complexity with the rest of the world about which we have nevertheless gone on to make coherent generalizations based on far from complete observations. We must extend a similar procedure to our subject and expound it with the same systematic rules that do not sacrifice the diversity.

A basic persistent trait of African societies is the importance of religion. It falls like a shaft of light across the entire spectrum of life, fused and undifferentiated at one end, and refracted and highly refined at the other. From casual, daily, and spontaneous contexts to somber, highly structured public occasions, it is the focus of elaborate and detailed interest. In art and ritual, in speech, work and leisure, in field, home and travel, on land or on water, in health and in sickness, in need and in contentment, religion occurs with authoritative force. African communities have consequently lived, moved, and had their being in religion.

Even the Greeks of classical antiquity noted this fact about Africa. Diodorus of Sicily, for example, a historian of the first century B.C., transmits a tradition from Homer about the religious reputation of the Ethiopians, enlarging it with a comment about the blacks being the first to honor the gods with sacrifices. The power of religion, he claims, protected them from falling victim to foreign invasion. He comments on how the sacrifices of the Ethiopians "are the most pleasing to heaven," as a consequence of which Homer in the Iliad represents both Zeus and the other gods going to Ethiopia to share in the religious festivities (Snowden 1970:146-47).

Of course, not all Western commentators, then or later, were as positive about the role of religion in African society, but all were struck by its pervasive presence, and on that fact alone it is sufficient to secure our argument.

The African reality is rooted in the religious paradigm and is expressed in a complexity of rituals and symbols which together pervade the entire field of human existence.[1] Religion clings to life and illuminates it from all angles, and Africans have used its power to create mansions of devotion and community, tempting some scholars to venture the theory that the life-affirming preoccupations of Africans suggest that religion is merely a pretext for a heroic humanism, whereas religion is essentially an affair of the dead (Zahan 1979). This theory misunderstands the African sense of religion as efficacious power which furnishes the worldview as well as the articulation of specific parts of that worldview to details of existence and experience.

It is possible, without a full account of any one religious tradition in Africa, to understand something of the character of the old gods as they encountered the new gods. It is important to conceive this encounter in terms of creative tension rather than as exclusive polarity.

The Christian dimension

Christianity reached Alexandria and Cyrene from Palestine during the first decades of the religion.[2] By the middle of the second century Christianity had spread along the North African coast, reaching there from Rome. The evidence is that sections of the indigenous population were converted and that some of them joined the ranks of the early martyrs. Several African converts appear on a list of people martyred in July A.D. 180. The Berber element was important in the church: St. Augustine (d. 430), for example, was almost certainly of Berber stock; his natal town, Thagaste, was a center of Berber culture, and his son's name, Adeodatus, "God-given," is emphatically un-Roman. One writer, Julian of Eclanum, dubbed Augustine as "the African sophist," so deeply African were his thoughts and feelings.[3]

What was the religion of the local population? This consisted largely of the worship of Saturn, also called Ba'al, whose symbols appeared in churches, and formulae associated with its worship were adopted by bishops. Even the term "Senex," a local religious title, was adopted by the church. Some of the ideas of Saturn-worship infiltrated Augustine's thinking, especially the notion of Saturn as capable of dark human passions and vengeance. Augustine wrote: "God orders man to love him, and threatens deep miseries if he does not do so," indicating the vengeful attribute of Saturn (Ferguson 1969:189). It has been suggested that even the passionate attachment to martyrdom was more likely a hangover of the deep-rooted tradition of human sacrifices. Tertullian, a second-century African Church Father, asserts that God does desire human blood and that some Christians provoked their enemies in order to make a sacrifice of themselves (Ferguson 1969:189).

The new God of Christianity was clearly arriving by the routes opened and traversed by the old gods and proceeding at a pace they had established. Often the two sets of gods surfaced in a frank acknowledgement of parallelism. A member of Augustine's congregation told him of his attachment to the old gods without that conflicting with his Christian profession. "Oh, yes," he confessed to Augustine, who was himself the supreme master of the art, "I go to idols; I consult seers and magicians, but I do not abandon God's church. I am a Catholic" (Ferguson 1969:189). Modern archeological excavations have established the existence of some 200 churches and chapels in Berber villages, suggesting the depth of Christian penetration beyond the Roman quarters of Carthage (Frend 1952:53). The proximity, then, to sources of indigenous assimilation could not have been closer. As one writer aptly put it, Christianity and its new gods "did not burst [upon Africa] like a clap of thunder, but stole into ears already prepared. Neither on her popular nor on her philosophic side was [Christianity] a creed apart" (Forster 1961:75).

In Ethiopia a similar development appears to have taken place. The institutionalized pagan religion of Ethiopia resulted from the presence of Sabean immigrants who crossed the Red Sea in about 1000 B.C. and later from an amalgamation of Graeco-Roman religious materials. Temples were erected at Yeha, Axum, Matera, and other places. The religion was based on a triune cult of the moon god, the sun goddess, and the morning star, a pattern clearly evocative of the Egyptian trinity of Isis, Osiris, and Horus. Though the names varied, especially after Greek gods were introduced, the main temples practiced a cult of three divinities. King Ezana (reigned A.D. 320-360), for example, before his conversion presided over the cult of Astar, Beher, and Meder. An important feature of the ancient religion was the integration of state and society with religion at the core. Consequently the king, assuming a divine status, was high priest as well as ruler and military commander. In inscriptions made by him, Ezana styles himself at one point as "King of kings, the son of the invincible god Ares" (Tafla 1967:29). Thus, as Diodorus observed of an earlier time, religion played a critical role in assuring the cohesion of society and the stability of the state.[4]

By the time Christianity was officially established in the fifth century, Ethiopia or areas in active contact with it had known the religion from the first decades of its existence, with Meroe as a possible source of influence. Much later, monophysite refugees fleeing the persecution unleashed by the Council of Chalcedon of 451 sought sanctuary in Ethiopia, itself in the monophysite camp, and thus added to the number of active Christians who helped to spread the religion.

It is clear in Ethiopia, too, that the new religion gravitated towards the most active centers of pagan worship and made use of the old gods to articulate the creed and to confirm an identical interest in healing and miracles. The old gods were therefore baptized, given Christian names, and invested with scriptural sanction. The tension that might occur from Christian expansion was averted by submitting Christian materials to the force of local paradigms. But, far from parodying the old religions, Christianity through translation initiated a strong renewal of Ethiopian culture, resulting in the efflorescence of Ethiopian literature. Translation of religious works fueled the spread of learning, language study, and the founding of schools. By A.D. 678 much of the translation work was completed.

Having succeeded in penetrating Ethiopian culture, the new religion was challenged to determine its final attitude to the old gods. This issue was never settled once and for all, so that in the modern period of Ethiopian history it was to surface as an unresolved phenomenon. In times of crisis, such as the abortive Italian invasion of 1896 and the later attack of 1935 by the Fascist regime of Mussolini, the spirit of the nation, knit of both old and new, reasserted itself to avert permanent ignominy. The Ethiopian rulers, laying claim to both temporal and spiritual power, defended the nation against external enemies, both European and Islamic. In the last of these external crises, the Ethiopian strongman, Haile Selassie, succeeded in ridding himself of the Italians. The invaders left in 1941. Diodorus may after all have a clue to the secret force of religion in Africa.

In spite of the doctrinal struggles of intervening centuries and the attempt to reform Ethiopian Christianity, the indigenous religious paradigms survived, not so much in opposition to the new gods as in subtle alliance with them. The rise of Islam in the seventh century served to isolate Christian Ethiopia from its successfully Islamized neighbors, and the old gods rose to add their share to a sense of

Ethiopian identity. The isolation from the outside world was deepened within Ethiopia itself by the absence of a central ecclesiastical structure, and that left the new gods at the mercy of indigenous infiltration. In the survival of the nation both forces had a stake and a contribution.

Christianity and colonialism

The close interplay between Christianity and indigenous culture should be borne in mind when we reflect on the historical coincidence between the nineteenth-century missionary movement and colonialism, and this led to a complicated relationship in which missionaries felt entitled to colonial support and backing on the one hand, and, on the other, where colonial administrators felt justified in incorporating missionary spheres into the empire.[5] Missionary objections, for example, to local custom, such as dancing, nakedness, or polygamy; religious practices such as sacrifice, mortuary rites, or drumming; and notions of witchcraft might be translated into administrative ordinance with legal force. Furthermore, the operation of missionary schools might be given government sanction, thus adding political authority to the use of schools as proselytizing agencies or as instruments of social control. One writer, describing one extreme example of missionary use of political power in what is now Zambia, says that the mission "turned a fortuitous assertion of theocratic prerogatives into a system of governmental authority" (Rotberg 1965:55).

Yet mission was not always viewed with favor by colonial administrations, whether in Africa or elsewhere.[6] Political alliances shifted radically, such as after World War I when German interests in Africa were sequestered. German missionary fortunes correspondingly declined, often with no adequate replacement by other countries.[7] In other places colonial administrations adopted a pro-Islamic policy which placed missions under severe restrictions. Furthermore, in areas where Christian schools operated, their success as instruments of conversion was limited, though they might open the way for other unforeseen changes. Thus we have a curious irony in the fact that most of the nationalist leaders were educated in Christian schools, a fact which modifies the idea of Christian education as collaboration with colonialism.

Another irony was the universal effect of vernacular translations and the literacy which accompanied the enterprise. In Ghana, for example, two organizations which promoted the cause of selfhood and thus contributed to national awakening were the Fante Confederation of the 1870s and the Reference Group of the 1880s. Both were led by national Christian figures, and both pressed for a greater role for Africans in public life. The Reference Group in fact campaigned for greater use of the vernacular in religious and social life (Bartels 1965:124),[8] an issue which the Basel Mission was to champion for rather different reasons. We also have, as early as 1905 following the Russo-Japanese War, an example of educated Christians taking a lead in forming political opinion. The editor of *The Gold Coast Aborigines* admonished the colonial power to learn from Russia's defeat at the hands of the Asian underdog, finding sanction for this piece of bold political prophecy in Jeremiah (Bartels 1965:159).[9]

I have elsewhere described in some detail the relationship, or what is assumed to be the relationship, between Christian mission and European colonialism (Sanneh 1989). Suffice it to say that Christian missionaries were responsible in most places for promoting translation, including the creation of vernacular alphabets, the production of grammars, dictionaries, and other linguistic materials with which the translation enterprise was supported. The effects on the wider culture cannot be overemphasized. One ironic effect was to undermine the logic of colonial overlordship by laying the basis for indigenous cultural nationalism. Even if some missionaries played an active political role as the religious vanguard of advancing gunboats, there were many others who turned their political influence to supporting the national cause against the imperial powers. One authority has observed in this connection that missionaries perceived in Western influences a threat to the interests of the African Church.

> During the modern period . . . the missionary world was conscious of being engaged, with only stationary or diminishing forces, against a steadily growing body of Western influences, whose operation was by no means necessarily favorable to the growth of African Christianity. . . . As at that time when their position has appeared to be threatened by the violent inroads of the Arabs, so now, missionaries

felt compelled to enter the political arena and to protect by wider than spiritual methods what they believed to be the interests of the African Church (Oliver 1952:247).

One fairly representative missionary figure, the German, J. Lewis Krapf, who served with the Church Missionary Society in East Africa, addressed some remarks to those of his colleagues who might be pinning their hopes on European colonial mastery of Africa to create the atmosphere favorable to the advance of Christianity. He wrote:

> Expect nothing, or very little from political changes in Eastern Africa. Do not think that because East Africans are 'profitable in nothing to God and the world' they ought to be brought under the domination of some European power, in the hope that they may bestir themselves more actively and eagerly for what is worldly and, in consequence, become eventually more awake to what is spiritual and eternal. On the contrary, banish the thought that Europe must spread her protecting wings over Eastern Africa, if missionary work is to prosper in that land. . . . Europe would, no doubt, remove much that is mischievous and obstructive out of the way of missionary work, but she would probably set in its way as many and, perhaps, still greater checks (Krapf 1860:512).

History confronts us with many paradoxes, but the paradox of mission as the unwitting stimulus for African nationalism deserves better understanding.[10] Under the seemingly suffocating heat of cultural imperialism, described so eloquently in one instance by Monica Wilson (1969:266), the spirits of the old gods, in consort with the new gods, discovered the conditions congenial to incubate a full-blown pride that some writers came to characterize as "Negritude."

African Christian independency

One spectacular result of the creation of the vernacular Scriptures was the emergence of prophet movements and African independent churches. With the availability of such Scriptures and the ability to read them in their mother tongue, Africans arrived at a powerful sense of their own indispensability for the enterprise from which mission had excluded them. The point of historical friction was the Niger Mission (1841-1891) which was led by Bishop Samuel Ajayi Crowther (c. 1807-1891). In untidy maneuvers to unseat Bishop

Crowther, the (Anglican) Church Missionary Society dismantled the Niger Mission, removing twelve of the fifteen African agents. This happened between 1880 and 1890. Crowther himself was replaced by European leadership. It added fat to the fire, and the African response flared in calls for separation from the mission. Before long the revolt spread to other missions, with the Baptists and Methodists joining the Anglicans in demanding separation.[11] The experience was repeated all over Christian Africa (Barrett 1968; 1982), and today we have more than 8000 such movements. "Independency" is the term employed to describe the phenomenon.

Independency represents Africa's unique contribution to the story of Christianity. It is the dramatic adaptation of new teachings to the African environment. The carriage of Christianity, bearing down on a straight line from the Western world, has been unscrambled to fit it out for the different terrain of Africa. It now rocks to the tune of colorful processions and their shouts of praise and song.

We may summarize the characteristics of independency as follows. The important religious agents remain the prophets, preachers, and healers; they mediate between the pull of the old and the push of the new. In their hands the vocabulary of salvation is made to conform to the grammar of kin obligation. In respect to themes, prayer, dreams, and healing occupied a prominent place in the origin and development of independency. As for goals, these might be described as power, community, and wholeness. Religion was more than a solitary affair for the African, and independency has demonstrated that social character to the fullest possible extent. It has also in this regard encouraged a rich and diverse manifestation in established standards of regalia, music, and dance. As a consequence Christianity is encountered in its vividness, its sounds and in movement, rather than as a processed cognitive system. Thus Christianity came to impinge on the entire spectrum of life in the manner of the old religions. In the successful assimilation of the new gods, therefore, we catch a luminous reflection of the old spirits, arrayed in creative alliance with the new rather than in inhibiting parody.

Islam and the African experience

Like Christianity before it, Islam made its appearance in Africa right from the beginning of its history. The accounts describe how the Prophet Muhammad dispatched a body of his followers to seek sanctuary in Christian Ethiopia following fierce persecution in Mecca (Ishaq 1967:146-53). Subsequently the Prophet and his companions (Arabic *ashab*) emigrated as a body to Medina in 622, a move that is called the *hijrah*. The next time Muslims appeared in Africa it was as a conquering army in 647; the Prophet had passed away in 632. Further military incursions followed, with one in 711 opening the way for the permanent establishment of the faith in North Africa, what the Arabs call Ifriqiya.

North Africa came to nurture its own brand of Islam with the extremist Kharijites, and, later, with the Fatimids whose rule spread from Egypt to Morocco. As Ibn Khaldun (d. 1406) was to demonstrate, Islam provided a successful framework for political integration and social cohesion of North Africa (Khaldun 1982). Two reform movements sprang up there in an effort to overturn isolationist pressures and rechannel local forces into the orthodox mainstream. One was the Almoravid (Ar. *al-murabitun*) movement led by Ibn Yasin (d. 1059), a devout, ascetic character resolved to remedy what he considered the scandalous ignorance of the Berbers of the most basic tenets of the religion they professed to follow. He swept over the area, sword in one hand and the Book in the other, waging a struggle of radical Islamization. He achieved astonishing success. But power spoiled the Almoravids, and their vision of a true Islam dimmed from the conflicting attractions of civilized splendor.

Then arose the Almohads (Ar. *al-muwahhidun*), literally, "monotheists," under the charismatic Ibn Tumart (d. 1130), who in 1127 claimed the title of Mahdi and launched a campaign to institute Sunni Islamic orthodoxy, repudiating anthropomorphism (*tajsim*) as heretical and upholding instead the principle of spiritual exegesis (*ta'wil*) of the Qur'an (Macdonald 1965:243-52). He denounced the Almoravids as corrupters of the faith and the scholars (*'ulama*) as their unholy allies. Stern and energetic, Ibn Tumart was a deeply learned man, a disciple of the famous al-Ghazali (d. 1111) but without the latter's supple resources. He carried his campaigns with utter ruthlessness, convinced he was the inaugurator of a fresh religious dispensation for his people.

However, Ibn Tumart outreached himself, and his successors were consumed by the demands of the far-flung Almohad empire, from the southern Sahara to the high ranges of Andalusian Spain. From the inevitable decline that came with political decay, Islam descended to the levels of the pre-reform era in which the synthesis of *fiqh* (law) and *zuhd* (ascetic practice) predominated over undiluted formalism.

Yet the legacy of the reformers did not die completely, and in many parts of West Africa enough was transmitted to prime the local Muslim temper with an ideological commitment of some kind to orthodox rectitude. Specific historical examples can be established quite readily. One of the most influential figures in West African Islam was 'abd al-Karim al-Maghili (d. 1505), and he came from North Africa, living in Songhay during the reign of Askiya Muhammad Ture (reigned 1493-1528), and supplying the askiya with religious arguments for Islamic reform (Hiskett 1962). Al-Maghili's views were known with approval to 'Uthman dan Fodio (d. 1807), the creator of the Sokoto Caliphate and three centuries removed from the earlier reformer. A recently discovered manuscript has also established firm links with Cairo from where al-Suyuti (1445-1505) (Sartain 1975), one of the most influential scholars of his day, gave out directives concerning the proper observance of Islam in West Africa (Hunwick 1970:7-33).[12] Clearly there was sustained contact, and one which helped Islam to leave a permanent imprint on African societies south of the Sahara.

Thanks to the infusion of reform ideas from beyond the Sahara, African Islam embodied an internal dynamism of a steady assimilation into the local setting on the one hand, and, on the other, a corresponding impulse to check uncritical syncretism. More than in African Christianity, in African Islam we come upon dramatic examples of a religious polarity between rampant syncretism and radical iconoclasm. The kind of synthesis we described of Christian and indigenous materials exists in Islam only as a potential for controversy, for Muslims, however ignorant of the sacred Arabic, are given no alternative for the observance of the ritual obligations.

A great deal has been written on this aspect of Islam in Africa which it would be impossible to try to reproduce here even in a bibliography. Consequently a few arbitrarily selected themes must suffice. The jihad wars, which carried to spectacular lengths the radical iconoclastic tendencies of Islam, achieved their greatest victories in Hausaland in the nineteenth century, with similar happenings in Masina, Adamawa, and Senegambia. But the dramatic nature of jihad should not mislead us about its enduring significance. The struggle to establish a reform ethos in Islam in other ways more peaceful was more representative of the history of the religion in Africa, and here the dialogue with the old gods was one of mutual influence. Jihad had undeniable importance for the subsequent direction of the local practice of Islam, as Mervyn Hiskett has strongly argued (1984:303). But it was no substitute for peaceful reform and expansion which, through the channels of education (*ta'lim*) and pilgrimage (*hajj*), outdistanced and outlived the reign of the sword (Wilks 1968:162-95).

The peaceful promotion of Islam encouraged greater collaboration with African religious agents. Muslim religious officials, such as *imams*, *qadis*, *'ulama*, *sharifs*, and others qualified as "men of God," evoked their counterparts in the indigenous culture.[13] The channels of this peaceful transmission of Islam included traders, trade routes, commercial centers, organized states, and the institutions that served them. Settled Muslim communities intermarried with local populations, and family bonds became bearers of Islamic influence.

In order to show how Islam first arrives at a convergence with the old Africa before it can strike on an independent course, I would like to consider a number of examples concerning the underlying indigenous perception to which the new religion is made to align itself. It is necessary for this reason to focus on religious agents, especially in their transitory capacity, much like visiting preachers or pilgrim caravans who left behind strong images which hardened with first impression.

Local cults and shrines have often been the center of activity for the blending of the old and new, and it is sometimes the case that religious agents in these settings may be lapsed Muslims or emancipated shrine priests; in either case both foster a rich sort of eclecticism. For example, one shrine priest (*kagbir-wura*) in Ghana offers two prayers morning and evening and fasts three days in the fast month of Ramadan. He carries a rosary, a copy of the Qur'an, and a bundle of Arabic manuscripts, although he himself cannot read Arabic at all (Levtzion 1968:66). Although the shrine-priest had come from a once-Muslim family, he now offers a mix of Islam and traditional religion, the kind of bridge that eased the path of transition. This helped maintain a certain rudimentary familiarity with Islam without implying a dramatic lurch towards formal conversion. Islam at this stage exists in the feelings of non-Muslims as a superimposition, much like batik, rather than as a principle of critical differentiation.

Another example concerns an itinerant Muslim cleric. In his case, too, he attaches his practice of Islam to the backdrop furnished by local religious materials. He is given the name of *alfa*. On one occasion in June 1945 the cleric appeared before an audience headed by the Paramount chief of a Mende chiefdom in Sierra Leone, West Africa. He spoke of a once-powerful chief who was seized on a walk and transported to heaven where he fell victim to searing hunger and "wept bitterly," realizing what hunger was like. Then the cleric spoke about the value of obedience to constituted political authority as a mirror of obedience to God. Then he went on to paint a particularly idyllic picture of heaven where, in some contradiction to his earlier assertion, there was no hunger or death or drowsiness. There was no darkness, only pure light. But it was also a place where sensuous desires were fulfilled, with the means available in inexhaustible abundance. Finally, the cleric asked the chief to make a sacrifice to ease his path to heaven. The food sacrifice consisted of a large quantity of seed-rice, cooked sweet potatoes, an old coat, a pair of sandals to protect the feet from thorn-pricks, two cocks, an old mortar and pestle, two pails, and a quantity of kerosene. These were to be contributed by the rich. The poor were to give a bundle of wood and seven bamboo slats, and the *alfa* himself, not to be outdone, would donate seven kola nuts, one old pot, and three splinters of wood.

Clearly this sacrifice belonged to the local religious tradition where the name for it is *kpakpa*, and that was the inspiration and the paradigm for the *alfa*'s action. Islam, at least initially, was not denying this or even competing with it. It was taking advantage of it, with a gentle hint that it can add the element of hope in a future life. In the meantime those who converted to Islam would continue to benefit by the providence of the old gods (Little 1946:111-13). The widespread use of amulets, charms, and other forms of instrumental religion in Muslim Africa indicates a deep level of indigenization, with Islam being transposed into local terms as a religion of power, whatever the scruples of the orthodox party.

In another example Islam came upon the Poro secret society in Sierra Leone. The Poro here again was better organized, more ably maintained, and better articulated in economic and political terms, and the consequence was Islam being reduced to a subordinate position without, of course, losing its separate identity. Poro and Islam came together when the local population decided on a campaign of economic boycott. Traditionally the people initiated this campaign by placing an interdiction on the harvesting of oil-palm, represented by a Poro medicine being left in the field. In this particular case Islam was incorporated into the arsenal of Poro by the inclusion of two wooden slates containing Arabic material in magic squares (*'ilm al-awfaq*), a combination that was believed to add greater potency. At this level, too, Islam is conceived to be in continuity with the old gods, following the direction in which they always pointed (Alldridge 1901: 133-34).

The reference to chiefs and authority brings us to an important theme in the domestication of Islam in Africa. Islam has always been attracted to organized societies, finding in local hierarchies a natural affinity for the institutions of its religious life. Here again the identity of interest which might exist would first occur on the level of indigenous customs. Among the Dagomba of Ghana, for example, there is a Damba festival which commemorates the birthday of the Prophet. Yet the chiefs who observe this ceremony are far removed from Islam, and the Damba has lost any connection with the mawlid of Islam. The festival is really "an occasion for sub-chiefs to pay homage to their senior chief. The Damba, more than any of the other Muslim feasts in Dagomba, is a chiefly affair" (Levtzion 1968:98). Islam is thus adopted, if at all, to bolster traditional political authority and add color to a local ceremony. Thus domesticated, the foreign religion exhibits the marks of local familiarity even though at an advanced stage of participation the earlier loyalties might be weakened. However, that advanced stage may remain in an indefinite future for a considerable number of people.

I have attempted to indicate the richness of the field in one example of the pacific tradition in African Islam, an example where clerical mediation has operated to offset any sharp break with the religion and spirituality of the old Africa (Sanneh 1979). All that material confirms that African destiny of the religion in its new environment. Without a central religious structure to direct practice and enforce a common code of faith and conduct, the incidence of local variation would remain very high indeed.

One further example throws an important light on the persistence of older religious attitudes even in exemplary Muslim communities. In March 1824 Hugh Clapperton, a Scottish Calvinist, arrived in Sokoto, the heart of the puritan revolution initiated by the Shehu Usuman dan Fodio (d. 1807) in north Nigeria. Clapperton was not a little disconcerted to find that the iconoclasm of the reformers had failed to change the outlook that provoked it in the first place. In a meeting with the son and heir to the Shehu, Muhammad Bello, Clapperton recounts with surprise the informed interest of the Sultan in matters arcane. "I first exhibited a planisphere of the heavenly bodies," he wrote. "The sultan knew all the signs of the Zodiac, some of the constellations, and many of the stars, by their Arabic names" (Bovill 1966:679). On a visit in the same city to the vizier of the Sultan, Clapperton appears to be pursued by a similar difficulty:

> This morning (April 9, 1824) I paid the gadado a visit, and found him alone, reading an Arabic book, one of a small collection he possessed. 'Abdallah,' he said, 'I had a dream last night, and am perusing this book to find out what it meant. Do you believe in such things?' 'No, my lord gadado; I consider books of dreams to be full of idle conceits. God gives a man wisdom to guide his conduct, while dreams are occasioned by the accidental circumstances of sleeping with the head low, excess of food, or uneasiness of mind.' 'Abdallah,' he replied, smiling, 'this book tells me differently' (Bovill 1966:695).

In one incident Clapperton himself became the subject of religious curiosity. He says,

> "I was unluckily taken for a fighi, or teacher, and was pestered, at all hours of the day, to write out prayers by the people. . . . Today my washerwoman positively insisted on being paid with a charm, in writing, that would entice people to buy earthen-ware of her; and no persuasions of mine could either induce her to accept money for her service, or make her believe the request was beyond human power" (Bovill 1966:669-70).

Lamin Sanneh

Thus even at the height of the reform movement in the Sokoto Caliphate, there was a strong tendency to recast the leading protagonists as medicine men in conformity with the older paradigm.

All these examples and others suggest that Islam is also involved in a subtle process of translation whereby it is brought within access of indigenous comprehension. Islamic gains in Africa are thus freighted with a considerable amount of indigenous values and attitudes, confirming the success of Africa in harnessing the power of the new gods to serve Islam's purposes.

Whatever the case regarding the untranslatability of the Qur'an and a correspondingly negative attitude towards the vernacular as *'ajami* (foreign), there is no doubt about the stimulating effect of the interaction of Islam and Christianity in Africa. Together both religions have contributed in their own ways to the pluralist heritage of Africa, and the challenge of contemporary Africa is to preserve that heritage against the pressures of doctrinaire statism and religious fundamentalism.

NOTES

1. The French Capuchin missionaries in West Africa were from the first go struck with the pervasive significance of religion in African life (Wiltgen 1956).

2. Apollos, a Jew born in Alexandria, "an eloquent man, and mighty in the Scriptures," was among the disciples at Ephesus. He is described as a leading Christian (Acts 18:24ff.). He would presumably have been one of the early pioneers of the church in Alexandria. In the heady days of the Christian movement of Pentecost we are told that there were people present from Cyrene in Libya (Acts 2:10). Cyreneans are also mentioned as being present at Antioch (Acts 11:20).

3. One authority speaks of Augustine's African roots thus: "Much of his thinking is centered on Africa; his sympathy for Carthaginian Dido, his rebuke of his compatriot Maurus for failing to understand his native country, and the whole approach of his greatest work, *The City of God*, which is curiously detached and seems to view the Roman Empire from the outside" (Ferguson 1969:184).

4. For the modern theme see Rubenson (1978:362, 366, 382, 394-95).

5. Roland Oliver (1952) gives a brilliant analysis of this theme.

6. One hapless lieutenant governor of Papua New Guinea was reportedly driven to suicide by the persistent criticism of a missionary. See Torben Christensen and William R. Hutchison, eds. (1982:25).

7. The case for Tanzania has been examined by Terence Ranger (1971:133-38).

8. For the Confederation, see Bartels (1965:88-90).

9. The text quoted from Jeremiah was: "Thus saith the Lord, Let not the wise man glory in his wisdom, neither let the mighty man glory in his might" (*The Gold Coast Aborigines* 1905:23).

10. A welcome note is sounded in E. A. Ayandele (1966).

11. For a summary of this subject, see Sanneh (1983).

12. Hunwick's critical edition of al-Maghili's *Responsa* is: *Sharica in Songhay: The Replies of al-Maghili to the Questions of Askia al-Hajj Muhammad* (1985).

13. Aspects of this question are treated extensively in Trimingham (1959) and in Sanneh (1979).

14. For aspects of religious pluralism in Africa, see Sanneh (1983:210-41).

REFERENCES

Alldridge, T. J.
1901   *The Sherbro and Its Hinterland*. London and New York: Macmillan.

Ayandele, E. A.
1966   *The Impact of Christian Missions on Modern Nigeria*. London: Longman.

Barrett, David B.
1968   *Schism and Renewal in Africa: An Analysis of Six Thousand Contemporary Religious Movements*. Nairobi: Oxford University Press.

Bartels, F. L.
1965   *The Roots of Ghana Methodism*. Accra: Cambridge University Press and Methodist Book Depot, Ltd.

Bovill, E. W., ed.
  1966   *Missions to the Niger, Vol. IV: The Bornu Mission 1822-25*. London: The Hakluyt Society Series II, Vol. 130.
Christensen, Torben, and William R. Hutchison, eds.
  1982   *Missionary Ideologies in the Imperialist Era: 1880-1920*. Denmark: Aros.
Ferguson, John
  1969   "Aspects of Early Christianity in North Africa," *Africa in Classical Antiquity*, ed. by L. Thompson and John Ferguson. Ibadan University Press.
Forster, E. M.
  1961   *Alexandria: A History and a Guide*. New York: Anchor Books.
Frend, W. H. C.
  1952   *The Donatist Church*. Oxford.
The Gold Coast Aborigines
  1905   *The Gold Coast Aborigines, Vol. 9*, no. 23.
Hiskett, Mervyn
  1962   "An Islamic Tradition of Reform in the Western Sudan from the 16th to the 18th Century," *Bulletin of the School of Oriental & African Studies*, 25(3).
  1984   *The Development of Islam in West Africa*. London: Longman.
Hunwick, John
  1970   "Notes on a Late 15th Century Document Concerning 'al-Takrur,' " *African Perspectives*, ed. by Christopher Allen and R. W. Johnson. Cambridge University Press.
  1985   *Sharica in Songhay: The Replies of al-Maghili to the Questions of Askia al-Hajj Muhammad*. London: Oxford University Press for the British Academy.
Ishaq, Ibn
  1967   *Sirat Rasul-u-llah*, ed. and trans. by Alfred Guillaume, *The Life of Muhammad*. Oxford (repr. Karachi, 1978).
Khaldun, Ibn
  1982   *Histoire des Berberes et des Dynasties Musulmanes de l'Afrique Septentrionale*, trans. by Le Baron de Slane, 4 vols. Paris.

Krapf, J. Lewis
    1860   *Travels and Missionary Labours in East Africa*. London.
Levtzion, Nehemia
    1968   *Muslims and Chiefs in West Africa: A Study of Islam in the Middle Volta in the Pre-colonial Period*. Oxford.
Little, Kenneth
    1946   "A Muslim Missionary in Mendeland," *Man*, Journal of the Royal Anthropological Institute, September-October.
Macdonald, Duncan B.
    1965   *The Development of Muslim Theology, Jurisprudence and Constitutional Theory*. Beirut: Khayat.
Oliver, Roland
    1952   *The Missionary Factor in East Africa*. London: Longman (repr. 1970).
Ranger, Terence
    1971   "Christian Independency in Tanzania," *African Initiatives in Religion*, ed. by David B. Barrett. Nairobi: East Africa Publishing House.
Rotberg, Robert I.
    1965   *Christian Missionaries and the Creation of Northern Rhodesia: 1880-1924*. Princeton University Press.
Rubenson, Sven
    1978   *The Survival of Ethiopian Independence*. London: Heinemann.
Sanneh, Lamin
    1979   *The Jakhanke: The History of an Islamic Clerical People of Senegambia*. London: The International African Institute.
    1979   "Muslims in non-Muslim societies in Africa," *Christian and Islamic Contributions Towards Establishing States in Africa South of the Sahara*. Stuttgart.
    1983   *West African Christianity: The Religious Impact*. Maryknoll, New York: Orbis Books.
    1989   *Translating the Message: The Missionary Impact on Culture*. Maryknoll, New York: Orbis Books.
Sartain, E. M.
    1975   *Jalal al-Din al-Suyuti*. Cambridge University Press.

Lamin Sanneh

Snowden, Frank M., Jr.
   1970   *Blacks in Antiquity*. Belknap Press, Harvard.
Tafla, Bairu
   1967   "The Establishment of the Ethiopian Church," *Tarikh*,
           Historical Society of Nigeria, 2(1).
Trimingham, J. Spencer
   1959   *Islam in West Africa*. Oxford.
Wilks, Ivor
   1968   "The Transmission of Islamic Learning in the Western
           Sudan," *Literacy in Traditional Societies*, ed. by Jack
           Goody. Cambridge University Press.
Wilson, Monica
   1969   "Co-operation and Conflict: the Eastern Cape Frontier,"
           *The Oxford History of South Africa, Vol. I, South Africa to
           1870*, ed. by Monica Wilson and Leonard Thompson.
           London: Oxford University Press.
Wiltgen, Ralph M.
   1956   *A Gold Coast Mission History: 1471-1880*. Techny, Illi-
           nois: Divine Word Publications.
Zahan, Dominique
   1979   *The Religion, Spirituality and Thought of Traditional
           Africa*, tr. by Kate E. Martin and Lawrence M. Martin.
           Chicago: University of Chicago Press.

Janet Hodgson
College of the Ascension, Birmingham
and University of Edinburgh

"Don't fence me in": some problems in the classification of African religious movements

One has only to look at the wealth of material in Harold Turner's *Bibliography of New Religious Movements: Black Africa* (1977) or to sift through the myriad files in his Centre for New Religious Movements in Primal Societies to appreciate his contribution in trying to bring order to the study of African religious movements. As he himself rightly indicates (1979: chs. 5, 7), the choice of terminology alone may well add to the confusion as political scientists, social anthropologists, and historians vie with students of religion to provide systems of classification with which to order their material. He argues persuasively for a multi-disciplinary approach which will bypass the problems caused by the "tunnel vision" of any one discipline; his defining of the term "new religious movements in primal societies" and his typology of modern African religious movements have both been important contributions to this end.

When Turner began work on his typology in the early 1960s he was well aware of the dangers of such an exercise. One of the problems is that while the typology is useful for the systematic study of the religious dimensions of the African data, many and varied manifestations of religious development do not fit such a classification. There is also the difficulty that even where efforts are made to incorporate the mobility of African movements within a typology of sociological form (Turner 1979:58-60), classifications relating to

83

structure must by their very nature be in danger of obscuring rather than clarifying the dynamics in the historical process of religious change. Turner has since tried to overcome this problem by proposing a model which shows various possible levels of interaction between Christianity and tribal religions and by distinguishing between first- and second-stage responses (1983:108). But even the use of the term "new" in relation to religious movements raises the risk of leading to an episodic sort of studies which will either be abstracted from the historical process, frozen in time, or governed simply by the pace of change.

The challenge now is to build on the foundation which Turner has so ably laid and to show how our present understanding of African religious movements must be broadened to incorporate the widest possible manifestations of religious life. In so doing I will draw on my study of the Ntsikana movement, which spans more than 200 years of religious and social change among the Xhosa-speaking people (Hodgson 1985). Reference will also be made to my present research which looks at the wide variety of movements initiated by African people within the Church of the Province of Southern Africa (Anglican) (Hodgson 1986a).

Ntsikana was born in Xhosaland about 1780 and died in 1821. This was a time of rapidly increasing socio-cultural disturbance among the Xhosa as they sought to stem the white advance on their land and their independence in a hundred years of war. Ntsikana had a traditional upbringing, inherited status as a councillor, and took two wives. Then in 1815 in his cattle byre he had a vision which he interpreted as a calling from God, rather than from the ancestors who were the usual focus of religious activity among the Xhosa. Further strange happenings that day at a wedding dance are said to have been the in-filling of the Holy Spirit. From this time on he collected together a small band of disciples who met twice daily for praise, prayer, and instruction in the word of God.

Early missionary influence is thought to have come from Dr. Johannes Vanderkemp in his brief ministry to the Xhosa at the turn of the century. Ntsikana's more biblical teaching undoubtedly comes from his contact with Joseph Williams at the Kat River mission between 1816 and 1818. But unlike later converts, Ntsikana remained, living among his people and articulating his new language of faith, together with its expression in ritual, in a Xhosa idiom. He never received church baptism but believed that his washing off of the red ochre from his body in the living water of a river was his own sort of baptism. This inspired his theology of God as Creator of new life.

In his fourfold typology of new religious movements in Black Africa, Turner classifies Ntsikana's movement as syncretist (1979:56). Here a movement is consciously and intentionally syncretistic in the sense that a new system is created "by borrowing both from the African primal and from the invasive traditions." But far from intending to be neither traditional nor Christian, as is typical of this group, the genius of Ntsikana was precisely that he evolved a genuine expression of African Christianity rooted in his people's traditions. Turner substituted the designation synthetist for syncretist in his later model, but the form remains the same (1983:107). A typology is at best only an approximate classification, but there are also problems in categorizing some of the other religious movements which Ntsikana spawned.

Ntsikana's innovations, assimilated from the new, included the regular meeting together of a nonkinship group for worship, the singing of hymns, prayer in the sense of communion with a personal and loving God, and teaching on salvation through faith in Christ. Continuity with the old was maintained by drawing on elements of the Xhosa tradition as the point of departure and carriers of change. The dialectic in this process is epitomized in Ntsikana's Great Hymn. The symbols and imagery which he used drew their power and authority from being rooted in the everyday experience of the Xhosa, such as fighting, hunting, and animal husbandry. But he gave them new meaning by planting them in the Christian context and focusing on the historical figure of Christ. The music was developed from a Xhosa wedding song, but it became a carrier of change by being sung with a Christian text, the first hymn of Xhosa. Similarly, the literary form was that of a traditional praise-poem, but the praise was of God as Creator, defender, and protector, not the ancestors or a chief. He was thus able to meet the existential and interpretative needs of those of his people who wished to come to terms with the new on their own terms.

Ntsikana's Christianity emphasized grace for change within the material and historical order. He was concerned with development rather than revolution. He thus provided a modus operandi for survival as one tradition was interpenetrated by another. But his prophecies show that he distinguished between the message and the messenger and warned his people against the white intrusion in their life as distinct from the word of God which they brought with them.

Ntsikana banded his followers together in a group which he called the Poll-headed, namely an ox without horns, because his belief in divine grace required them to discard their weapons. They had to arm themselves spiritually by singing his hymns and submit to persecution on all sides, from black and white alike.

Certainly Ntsikana's following qualifies as a new religious movement as defined in Turner's terms (1983:103). It is definitely new, belonging neither to the primal religion nor the mission church. It is a creative religious response of the indigenous people to the gospel, and it is undoubtedly Christian. Some would classify it in Turner's fourth category of independent church, the first in South Africa (1979:57). But it does not spring from a parent orthodox church like the Ethiopian sub-type, nor does it incorporate healing or other overt manifestations of the Spirit as in the Zionist group. And even though revelation is involved, Ntsikana is seen as a prophet of the classical biblical type, standing on the edge of a growing tradition and affirming God's action in the historical process, rather than as some necromancer or crystal ball-gazer. The distinctive Christology of the movement does not allow it to fit into Turner's Hebraist category either, with its Old Testament emphasis.

In contrast to Ntsikana, his contemporary and rival, Nxele, developed a thaumaturgic doctrine which incorporated Christian symbols of the apocalyptic kind within his old world of reference. His prophecies were an attempt to manipulate the divine powers to the purposes of humans, thus drawing upon the power symbols of the new tradition in order to bring about that which he prophesied. Radical discontinuity constituted his understanding of divine intervention, and he became a symbol of militant resistance to the Xhosa. Turner rightly classifies this movement in his neo-primal category, but it must be remembered that Nxele had moved here from primal religion via the syncretist position.

The marginal people, misfits, outcasts, and refugees were among those who took the third option of rejecting the African symbol set and embracing the Christian one in the totality of its Western cultural package as found in the mission churches. But even though Ntsikana's disciples followed his instructions to join the newly established mission at Chumie after his death, they remained as a group apart, being known as "the congregation of the God of Ntsikana." In no sense was this an "internal revival" as allowed for in Turner's typology. Rather, it was an indigenous movement contained within the mission church which managed to keep its independent African identity through the regular singing of Ntsikana's Great Hymn and the fostering of an oral tradition concerning his prophecies and teaching.

Soga, a leading disciple of Ntsikana, moved to Chumie with the rest of the group. But he was a leading councillor to the paramount of the western Xhosa and a polygamist and insisted on remaining apart from the mission. He was in the forefront of social change in that he was the first Xhosa to plough, the first to irrigate his own lands, and the first to participate in the Western market production economy. Moreover, he often attended church on Sunday and gave up some Xhosa customs. At the same time he refused to be baptized and would consult a diviner in times of misfortune. He also retained his traditional political role and took an active part in three consecutive wars against the whites. He was a thorough Xhosa nationalist, and Ntsikana provided him with the necessary integrated symbols to worship God in an African way. He maintained Ntsikana's pattern of twice-daily services and would allow no other hymns but Ntsikana's to be sung, not even those of his mission-educated sons. This seems to fit Turner's syncretist/synthetist category, although it was never formalized in a movement (Hodgson 1986b).

Dukwana, the younger of Ntsikana's two sons, became totally absorbed into the mission framework of functioning, which equated Christianity with Western civilization and loyalty to the British Crown. He became the leader of the School people at Chumie, the first printer and the first elder. After working as an evangelist for fifty years at Chumie and then at Mgwali, he scandalized settler society by leaving the mission to fight for his paramount chief in the ninth and last of the Xhosa-Cape frontier wars in 1877-78 (Hodgson 1986b).

Dukwana fought for the right to be both a Christian and a Xhosa patriot. While actively participating in guerrilla warfare he held services for his people in the Pirie Bush in which Ntsikana's Great Hymn was sung together with Psalm 23. He maintained that he would be forever grateful for the benefits which Christianity and civilization had brought him, more especially the gift of salvation. But he was against the English because they had robbed the Xhosa of their country and were destroying them as people (Hodgson 1986b). He died defending his chief. As a secession from a mission church, Dukwana's movement would have become the first Ethiopian-type Xhosa independent church but for his untimely death.

Ntsikana's disciples were among the first literate Xhosa, and their writing down of his story helped to perpetuate the living tradition. Elsewhere I have shown how the constant interaction between the oral and written sources in each succeeding generation added prestige to the symbolic role of Ntsikana as a historic prophetic figure (Hodgson 1986c). This continued to fuel the growth and development of Ntsikana movements both within and without the mainline churches. However, for all the hagiography of the oral and written traditions, Ntsikana never becomes exalted as a messiah, and nowhere do we find the formation of a messianic-type independent church, as identified by Turner, which can no longer be really called Christian (1979:101-03).

On his deathbed Ntsikana directed his people to remain as firmly united as a ball of scrapings from a tanned hide (*ngenje mbumba yamanyama*), which forms an unbreakable mass when dry. This phrase came to mean "unity is strength" and became a powerful integrating symbol as from the end of the nineteenth century on, successive groups of Xhosa School people sought to draw on Ntsikana in seeking legitimation for the growth of Xhosa nationalism.

Apart from the more political orientation of the various Imbumba movements, the St. Ntsikana Memorial Association can be regarded as a move towards a civil religion. It was founded in 1909 as a Xhosa unity movement within a Christian context. The aim was to follow

Ntsikana in a consciously African approach to the new, which married progress with the rediscovery of Xhosa culture, customs, and history in a nonviolent tradition of evolutionary change. Ntsikana was represented as the first Xhosa saint, his call being compared with the directness of the revelation to Paul on the road to Damascus. Xhosa Christians were urged to forget their denominational differences and to unite as a black nation to fight white domination and oppression. The move was from a denominational aggregation, as defined by the white church, to an ethnic aggregation as defined by black Christians. Again this is a new religious movement which remains within the ambit of the mission church except that it crosses church boundaries. Not surprisingly, many of its leaders were also active in the African National Congress over the years. The St. Ntsikana Order of True Africans was another nationalist group which sought wider African unity.

In recent years the Ciskei President, Lennox Sebe, has attempted to redirect the power of Ntsikana as a symbol of national unity in Ciskei. He has banned the celebrations of the rival Mfengu and Xhosa organizations and has developed Ntaba kaNdoda, a mountain near King William's Town, as a national shrine and symbolic focus for Ciskei civil religion. The idea came from the Israeli national shrine at Masada, but Ntsikana provides the symbolic legitimation (Hodgson 1987).

The Ntsikana Memorial Church, founded by Burnet Gaba, the great-grandson of Ntsikana, as a breakaway from the United Free Church of Scotland in 1911, is a typical Ethiopian-type independent church except that the focus is on following in the footsteps of Ntsikana. Here the same symbols are at work as in nationalism, but different aspects are emphasized within the pietistic context to establish an African family church. Also a number of Zionist-type churches such as the Order of Ethiopia in Zion, Bishop Limba's Church of Christ, and E. Sigcu's "Church of Christ for the Union and Protection of Bantu Customs which is the Ntsikana Memorial," founded in 1922, incorporate Ntsikana's symbolic influence.

In following the Ntsikana tradition up to the present we have seen that African religious movements cannot be studied in isolation as discrete entities which are self-explanatory. Research has shown the importance of identifying new movements as part of an ongoing and continuous process of religious and social change set within a specific socio-political, economic, and historic context. Any typological classification must somehow take into account the dynamics of the processes which gave the movements birth and which continue to shape their development.

The Ntsikana material has also shown a constant seeking after integrating symbol with experience and experience with symbol, so that symbol rather than structure becomes a significant methodological focus. Symbols are dynamic, and the flow of symbols must be followed so as to see how different religious aggregations use symbols in seeking legitimation which will meet the pressing needs of life. The question one would ask of a situation is who is seeking to take over, or to offer, what symbols for the legitimation or motivation of what purpose, and from whence the symbols draw their power in the ever-changing tradition (Hodgson 1986d).

Symbol flow can take place in four different ways. Obviously old symbols can retain their original meaning. Then new symbols may be taken on which are soon filled with old meanings, as where Christian symbols acquire an African interpretation as with Nxele. At the same time old symbols can come to serve new purposes as is shown by Ntsikana's theology in the Great Hymn. A fourth possibility is that new symbols are grafted on which initially have little meaning to the receptor culture, as was the case with most of the first mission converts. The symbols are espoused because they are seen to have advantages, and only gradually do they take on the meaning of the groups who have acquired the symbol.

These insights might well provide a basis for a new system of classification. But whatever the case may be, a typology must embrace the widest possible variety of religious development as part of a historical continuum. This is abundantly clear when we look at the new religious movements within some of the mainline (historical/mission/older) churches. Like the independent churches, they have been "founded by Africans, for Africans to worship in African ways and to meet African needs as Africans themselves feel them" (Turner 1979:10). But here the indigenization process has been contained within the mainline church, as is shown by a study of the African contribution to the Anglican Church in Southern Africa. This process is not necessarily revivalistic by nature, nor does it lead to indigenous autonomous churches as allowed for in Turner's classifications (1979/1983).

Some of the Anglican movements are highly structured, like the African Mothers' Union and the Bernard Mizeki Men's Guild. Although the Mothers' Union is affiliated with the parent body in England, the African women have made the movement their own by having distinctive uniforms and functioning in a specifically African way with their own songs and ways of singing them, emphasis on prayer and preaching, special modes of fundraising, and all-night revival services. The Bernard Mizeki Guild is an evangelistic movement founded by migrant workers in the Western Cape in the early 1970s, which has now spread countrywide. It was named after the Mashonaland martyr who died in 1896. The men also have a special dress and an African mode of functioning quite unlike anything in the formal church.

The Order of Ethiopia is a unique example of an independent church that was formally incorporated into the Anglican fold in 1900. It has continued to function independently within the mother body with its own church buildings, its own priests, and its own mode of organization and worship. The Order now even has its own Anglican bishop, who is the grandson of the founder. There have been schisms over the years, but the main body remains an integral part of the Anglican Church.

Iviyo Lofakazi Bakakristu (The Legion of Christ's Witnesses) is a predominantly Zulu-speaking Anglican renewal movement founded by two priests in 1948. Iviyo is charismatic in nature, with great stress being laid on the gifts and the power of the Holy Spirit. But it also manifests a strong emphasis on evangelism and holiness as well as incorporating elements of Anglo-Catholicism. Over the years Iviyo has had to overcome opposition within the church because of fears of its independent leanings and incipient Zionism, but it continues to grow in strength and is spreading beyond the Zulu-speaking dioceses (Shorten 1984).

Mrs. Paul's prayer movements in Transkei, iNdaba zoSindiso (News of Salvation), falls midway in the spectrum of Anglican African initiative in that it was never formally organized but obtained the church's blessing. Mrs. Paul claimed to have received baptism in the Holy Spirit in 1950 and subsequently developed among the Xhosa a powerful healing ministry based on prayer. She was licensed by her bishop in 1961 but died in a car accident three years later. Her movement has continued, albeit in schismatic form, and thousands of church people come from all over the country to the annual commemorative festivals at Tsolo, as well as meeting regularly on the Reef. Other prayer and healing movements founded by black Anglicans from time to time have not received official recognition, but their amazing popularity shows that the immediate needs of African people are not being met by the church.

The annual church pilgrimages, which also attract large numbers of black Anglicans, are fairly unstructured and have cultic overtones. The June celebrations at the Bernard Mizeki shrine in Zimbabwe are attended by large numbers of Mothers' Union women, while the July pilgrimage to the shrine of the virgin martyr Manche Masemola in Sekhukhuneland, Transvaal, draws young and old among the north Sotho.

An even stronger and totally unstructured cult has grown up around the holy places associated with the southern Sotho prophetess and rain doctor Mantsopa (c. 1805-1906) at the Anglican mission at Modderpoort in the eastern Orange Free State. Although Mantsopa was baptized a Christian, her mystic associations belong to the Sotho-Tswana tradition. Nonetheless, the cave chapel, her grave, and a spring at the mission are places of pilgrimage for Anglicans and other African Christians throughout the year, and the annual Cave Sunday service is popular.

None of these particular prayer movements or prophet cults are exclusive, but Anglicans predominate. The heroic figures are clearly significant symbols of black identity for their followers, providing them with a way of being directly linked with God in their continued situation of oppression and suffering in South Africa. What is certain is that a specific set of symbols must authenticate itself in daily life in order to have authority.

The Umgalelo voluntary associations offer an example of African Christian initiative within ordinary parish life. These are mutual aid societies, such as burial and savings societies, which have taken on a religious orientation and could be regarded as a new category of independent church. Here business matters are sandwiched in the middle of a religious service, which Anglicans regard as "going to church" (Kokoali and Hodgson 1986).

The flexibility of the Anglican Church in containing the rich diversity of these new religious groupings would seem to stem from the universality of its symbols. The more rigidly structured mainline churches with congregational symbols are more likely to reject such initiatives, so leading to secessions. Comparative material in other parts of the Anglican Communion such as the Solomon Islands and Guyana (see Turner 1984:107), East Africa, Nigeria, Papua New Guinea, and New Zealand provide other striking examples of new movements incorporated within the church.

In such a situation any demarcation to increase clarity is in danger of obscuring the full spectrum of religious development, if not entirely destroying entities. African religious movements must be seen as part of a dynamic whole within their historical context. Scholars trained in the Western tradition must guard against the problems inherent in allowing structures imposed by the incoming culture to dominate their thinking and to decree their classifications.

REFERENCES

Hodgson, Janet

1985   *Ntsikana: History and Symbol: Studies in a Process of Religious and Social Change Among Xhosa-speaking People*. Ph.D. dissertation, University of Cape Town.

1986a   "New Movements Within the Anglican Church." Paper presented to the NERMIC Congress, University of the Witwatersrand.

1986b   "Soga and Dukwana: the Christian Struggle for Liberation in Mid 19th Century South Africa," *Journal of Religion in Africa* 16(3).

1986c   "Fluid Assets and Fixed Investments: 160 Years of the Ntsikana Tradition, Oral Tradition and Literacy," ed. by R. Whitaker and E. Sienaert, University of Natal, Durban.

1986d   "The Symbolic Entry Point: Removing the Veil of Structure from the Study of New Religious Movements," *Religion Alive: Studies in the New Movements and*

Janet Hodgson

Indigenous Churches in Southern Africa, ed. by G. C.
Oosthuizen. South Africa: Hodder and Stoughton.

1987   "Ntaba kaNdoda: Orchestrating Symbols for National
Unity in Ciskei," *Journal of Theology for Southern
Africa*, 58.

Kokoali, C., and Hodgson, J.

1986   "Mutual Aid Societies, Another Kind of Independency
and the Church." *Religion Alive*.

Shorten, R.

1984   "Iviyo Lofakazi Bakakristu: A Study of a Renewal Move-
ment in the Church of the Province of Southern Africa's
Diocese of Zululand." M.A. dissertation, University of
Cape Town.

Turner, Harold W.

1977   *Bibliography of New Religious Movements in Primal
Societies, Vol. 1: Black Africa*. Boston: G. K. Hall & Co.

1979   *Religious Innovation in Africa: Collected Essays on New
Religious Movements*. Boston: G. K. Hall & Co.

1983   "A Further Frontier for Mission: A General Introduction
to New Religious Movements in Primal Societies,"
Missionalia 11(3).

1984   "Reflections on African Movements During a Missiological Conference," *Missionalia* 12(3).

Joseph C. Chakanza
University of Malawi

New religious movements in Malawi: a bibliographical review

Recent studies in new religious movements in Malawi have revealed that its literature covers mainly the period between 1900 and 1940. The major movements discussed are broadly:
a) John Chilembwe's Providence Industrial Mission and Elliot Kamwana's Watch Tower movement;
b) secessions from the Livingstonia Mission of the Free Church of Scotland;
c) those introduced from southern Africa by labor migrants and others propagated by them from outside Malawi;
d) the offshoots of Joseph Booth's missionary activities;
e) anti-witchcraft movements.

After 1940 there is a dearth of material, apart from some account of independent churches and neo-primal movements in the Mulanje District of southern Malawi. In this discussion, I shall review select primary documents and historical and regional studies relevant to Malawi and evaluate their main orientations.

Unpublished sources

A widely-cited document held by the Malawi National Archives in Zomba is "The Historical Survey of Native Controlled Churches Operating in Nyasaland" compiled by M. C. Hoole for the Police Records. It is the earliest attempt, to my knowledge, at putting together the available information on known independent churches in Malawi up to 1940. Twenty-two churches are listed, though not in chronological order, with a few details concerning their origins, leaders, and activities. In the aftermath of the Chilembwe Rising of

1915, churches controlled by Africans came to be viewed by the administration as potential movements resistant to colonial rule. Therefore stringent regulations were laid down to check and control their activities. Naturally, the police material shows exclusive concern with the political orientations that the movements portrayed.

Since 1969 a few writers have attempted to draw up lists of independent churches in Malawi. R. J. Macdonald's "Chronological List of Independent Churches in Malawi Till 1940" (1969) is based on the document just discussed. J. M. Schoffeleers' "Provisional Listing of Independent Churches in Malawi" (1975)[1] records 82 churches. J. C. Chakanza's *Annotated List of Independent Churches in Malawi* (1980) gives 105, and the 1983 revised edition of the same work gives 135. Forty-one churches are recorded in J. B. Shelburne's "Namikango Church Survey 1978-79" (1980).

Apart from lists of independent churches, there are some unpublished works on specific movements from the research carried out by the University of Malawi's history, sociology, and religious studies departments and other interested parties. While the history and sociology papers concentrate on factual accounts according to their disciplines, the papers from the Department of Religious Studies have attempted to examine specifically religious issues such as doctrine, rites, and church administration. J. C. Chakanza's "A General Survey of Independent Churches in Malawi 1900-1979" (1979), an M. Litt. thesis, laid a foundation for his doctoral thesis, "Continuity and Change: A Study of New Religious Movements in Malawi 1900-1981" (1985). In these two works the author pieces together much of the information which has for a long time remained scattered. The long appendices which have been published separately give a clear idea of what still remains to be known about new religious movements in Malawi. Besides the historical facts, the author has advanced a broader and more general interpretation of the phenomenon of religious independence in Malawi. He considers the problem of defining religious independence the interconnection between religion and the wider society, the place on time scale, and the place in the total religious context.

From among the founders of independent churches in Malawi, a much treasured manuscript of historical value is Yesaya Zerenji Mwasi's "My Essential and Paramount Reasons for Working

Independently," dated July 12, 1933. It was read by Mwasi himself on the occasion he broke away from the Livingstonia Mission to found the Blackman's Church which is in Tongaland. This document has been described as "one of the most eloquent and cogently argued pleas for independency in the written records of the African Independent Churches" (Sources 1980:1). In 1975 the African Ancestors Religion, an anti-Christian movement, started releasing a series of documents under the general title: *Kubadwanso kwa makolo achikuda* (*The Rebirth of African Ancestors*).[2] Christianity is rejected because it is alien to the African people. The authors advocate a return to the ancestral way of worship. Although there is much that can still be collected to build up a corpus of primary sources, our hope rests with the success of the project, "History of Independent Churches," launched by the Malawi National Archives in 1980. The Organization of African Independent Churches (OAIC) secretariat in Nairobi has recently appealed to leaders of independent churches to start writing down histories of their churches. The response to this appeal in Malawi is not yet clear.

Published sources

There has not as yet been any bibliography of new religious movements in Malawi. However, a most commendable compilation of the Malawi sources is to be found in H. W. Turner's *Bibliography of New Religious Movements in Primal Societies: Vol. 1, Black Africa* (1977) which carries an annotated list of 51 books and published articles. By far the most publicized single movement is John Chilembwe's Providence Industrial Mission with 37 out of the 51 references. Among the missionary records which have usually assigned peripheral place to independent churches, the *Livingstonia News* carries valuable information on African-led churches between 1900 and 1916, particularly the Watch Tower movement which started in the Livingstonia Mission's sphere of influence.

Since the mid 1950s scholarly works on religious independence in Malawi and the neighboring territories have appeared. In a pioneering article, "The Politics of an African Separatist Movement in British Central Africa, 1892-1916" (1954:233-46), G. Shepperson views religious independence broadly as an interplay between internal factors such as colonial rule and the impact of mission education, and external factors, particularly the movement towards black autonomy in southern Africa from the turn of the century. G. Shepperson and T. Price's monumental work, *Independent African: John Chilembwe and the Origins, Setting and Significance of the Nyasaland Native Rising of 1915* (1958), stands out as a classic biography of a single founder of an independent church in Malawi.

On the Livingstonia secessions, R. J. Macdonald has discussed the independent churches' efforts to establish schools and their relation to the Livingstonia Mission and the colonial government in his article, "Religious Independency as a Means of Social Advancement in Northern Nyasaland in the 1930s" (1970:106-29). K. Lohrentz's "Joseph Booth, Charles Domingo and the Seventh-day Baptists in Northern Nyasaland" (1971:461-80) shows the influence of the enigmatic Joseph Booth in northern Malawi through his protegé, Charles Domingo. By far the most lucid account of religious independence within the Livingstonia Mission's sphere of influence is K. J. McCracken's *Politics and Christianity in Malawi 1875-1940* (1977). The author has a chapter on the background causes of the early secessions. He singles out the Mission's retrogressive policy especially after the first 25 years of evangelization. Issues which generated tension between the missionaries and their converts were polygamy, beer-drinking, traditional dancing, and the slow pace of handing over power to Africans. This last point is illustrated by J. K. Parratt's "Y. Z. Mwasi and the Origins of the Blackman's Church" (1978:193-206).

On the role played by Malawians in disseminating religious independence in the neighboring countries, Monica Wilson discusses the early origins of the African National Church which entered southern Tanzania from northern Malawi in the second part of her *Communal Rituals of the Nyakyusa* (1959).

Terence Ranger's "Early History of Independency in Southern Rhodesia" (1964:52-74) discusses the role played by Malawians in establishing the Watch Tower and Apostolic churches in Zimbabwe. In another article, "Christian Independency in Tanzania" (1971:122-45), Ranger singles out a few Malawian churches, such as the African National Church and the Last Church of God and His Christ, which entered Tanzania during the inter-War period. The ministry of a Livingstonia-trained Malawian who turned Watch

Tower preacher in south-central Zambia, Tomo Nyirenda, has been discussed by Ranger in "The Mwana Lesa Movement of 1925" (1975:45-75). Sholto Cross's "A Prophet Without Honour: Jeremiah Gondwe" (1970:171-84) is a case study of a Watch Tower community in Zambia. Some of the independent churches in Malawi have their roots in Zimbabwe and South Africa. M. L. Daneel in *Old and New in Southern Shona Independent Churches* (1971, 1974) discusses the origins of the Maranke Apostles and Masowe Apostles who have communities in Malawi. B. Jules-Rosette more specifically described the beliefs, practices, and hierarchical structure of the church of Yohane Maranke in her book, *African Apostles* (1975). She traces her own conversion and membership in the church and her attempt to introduce it to the United States of America. There is little about Maranke himself and the history of the church. Theological issues are not discussed; the book introduces only a labyrinth of legalistic practices. In *The Korsten Basket Makers* (1978) Dillon-Malone gives a penetrating account of the Masowe Apostles through their pilgrimage in southern Africa and East Africa. There is a deep mystery surrounding Masowe's hidden life. B. Sundkler's *Bantu Prophets in South Africa* (1948, 1961) and his *Zulu Zion* (1976) give an invaluable background to the understanding of the Zion churches in Malawi which were introduced from South Africa. D. B. Barrett's *Schism and Renewal in Africa* (1968), gives a survey of 250 tribes in sub-Sahara Africa, isolating factors that correlate with the emergence of independent churches in order to account for their rise and to predict future movements. He plots their growth and their successes but not their failures and inadequacies.

Some historians have studied religious independence in Malawi as an integral part of sociopolitical development. B. Pachai in "The State of the Churches in Malawi During the Early Protectorate Rule" (1972:7-27) discusses the tensions in the interaction between mainstream Christianity, independent churches, Islam, and local cults. In another work, *Malawi: History of the Nation* (1973), Pachai has a special section on the role of independent churches which stress their social and political motives, with hardly any sustained attempt at analysis. In the series, *Great Malawians to Remember* (1975-76), D. D. Phiri has published the biographies of two founders of independent churches. One title reads: *Charles Chidongo*

Joseph C. Chakanza

Chinula (1975) and the other *John Chilembwe* (1976). Religious independence is not an issue of particular interest to the author. Rather, these founders are seen in terms of their political or nationalist achievements within their church settings.

An attempt to classify the independent churches in Malawi has been made in J. K. Parratt's article, "Religious Independency in Nyasaland: A Typology of Origins" (1979:183-200). The author proposes to formulate a typology of origins. However, he merely ends up with identifying the different origins of churches, and a typology does not emerge.

On neo-primal cults, Audrey I. Richards' "A Modern Movement of Witch-finders" (1950:448-61) discusses the Mehape movement which swept Central Africa to Zaire from 1930. The Bwanali-Mpulumutsi movement in southern Malawi has been narrated by M. G. Marwick in "Another Modern Anti-witchcraft Movement in East Africa" (1950:100-112). Alison Redmayne's "Chikanga: An African Diviner with an International Reputation" (1970:103-28) gives an account of a famous medicine man in northern Malawi.

Publications from leaders of independent churches are few. The African National (International) Church has a 24-page document entitled: *The Constitution and Rules of the African National Church*. A section on "Belief" reads: "Africa is in need of a church that would correspond with her God-given customs and manners" (n.d.:1). Wikilifi Chimawo's *Chiyambi cha Mpingo wa Zion* (*The Origins of the Zion Church*) (1979) gives a dramatic account of the founder of Kamenya-Zion Church, Fanueli, who experienced a call to the healing ministry in 1930.

Regional studies

The only full-scale regional study to date is Wishlade's *Sectarianism in Southern Nyasaland* (1965). The author, an anthropologist, compares two areas in southern Malawi, the Mulanje District and Chapananga's chiefdom in Chik'wawa District, in order to identify and distinguish some factors prevalent in the formation of sects. He observes that in Mulanje there is a proliferation of sects, while Chapananga's area has none. This high incidence of sectarianism in Mulanje is accounted for by the lack of opportunities in the politico-administrative system due to the high density of population. He puts forward the thesis that ecclesiastical organization provides the means of acquiring followers for those unable to do so in other spheres. In Chapananga's area this can still be within the traditional political context. Although he refers to the whole country in his chapter on the origins of the sects, most of the book is based on his own field work in Mulanje District and Chapananga's area. His thesis is not supported by sufficient data, and he agrees in the end that it cannot be carried too far. He also admits that he had not been able to study in greater depth the sects in their religious dimension, as this aspect is beyond his competence.

Concluding observations

I have noted earlier that the period covered by most of the published works on Malawi's new religious movements falls mainly between 1900 and 1940. The Chilembwe era (1900-1915) covering the activities of Joseph Booth, Elliot Kamwana, and Charles Domingo has the greatest bulk of literature, understandably due to the political implications associated with it, reaching its climax in the 1915 Rising led by Chilembwe himself.

The Malawi Diaspora era (1920-1940) covers the activities of Malawians and their interaction with other peoples in neighboring countries. From the turn of the century, Malawians have traveled to the mining areas and farm lands in Zimbabwe and South Africa, Zambia, Tanzania, and Mozambique. While in southern Africa, many Malawians joined the Africa-led churches which inspired them. When they returned home, they introduced these churches among their own people. In this context the published works on religious movements in southern Africa form an important and indispensable basis for understanding the movements imported into Malawi from that region. The case with Zambia, Tanzania, and Mozambique is different insofar as hardly any movements from these countries have been introduced into Malawi. A number of religious movements which started in Malawi--independent churches such as the Last Church of God and His Christ and the Watchman Healing Mission, and neo-primal movements such as Bwanali-Mpulumutsi and Chikanga--gradually found their way into these countries. Published works on expansion of these movements refer to Malawi as their *fons* (source) if not *origo* (origin).

Joseph C. Chakanza

In the post-War era, there have been hardly any significant secessions from mainstream churches in Malawi. But many independent churches have experienced secessions about which little has been written. Published works dealing with this period concentrate on neo-primal movements which have attracted many people.

Apart from Shepperson and Price's *Independent African*, Malawi does not yet have detailed published works such as H. W. Turner's study of the Church of the Lord (Aladura) and B. Sundkler's *Bantu Prophets* on individual or groups of religious movements.

Furthermore, studies such as Wim van Binsbergen's *Religious Change in Zambia* (1981) on religious change have not yet been carried out on a large scale. The task that lies ahead for the researcher in Malawi is to analyze convincingly forms of missionary or independent Christianity against the context of evolving economic and political structure of colonial and post-colonial society, and to make the link with non-Christian religious forms.

NOTES

1. I am grateful to Professor J. M. Schoffeleers for showing me this text.
2. Some of the documents in this series are:
   a. The Truth about Jesus, Saviour of the White People.
   b. The Demise of Christianity in Africa.
   c. The Jesus (Political) Party.
   d. The Death of Jesus Called Christ, in Jerusalem, Judea.
   e. The Worship and Rites of the African Ancestors.

REFERENCES

African Ancestors Religion
   1975   *Kubadwanso kwa makolo achikuda*.
African National (International) Church
   n.d.   *The Constitution and Rules of the African National Church*.
Barrett, D. B.
   1968   *Schism and Renewal in Africa*. Nairobi and London: Oxford University Press.

van Binsbergen, Wim
   1981   *Religious Change in Zambia*. London: Kegan Paul International.

Chakanza, Joseph C.
   1979   "A General Survey of Independent Churches in Malawi, 1900-1979." University of Aberdeen.
   1980   "Annotated List of Independent Churches in Malawi," *Sources for the Study of Religion in Malawi*. Department of Religious Studies, University of Malawi, nos. 3 and 8.
   1985   "Continuity and Change: A Study of New Religious Movements in Malawi, 1900-1981." University of Oxford.

Chimawo, Wikilifi
   1979   *Chiyambi cha mpingo wa Zion*. Lilongwe, Malawi.

Cross, Sholto
   1970   "A Prophet Without Honour: Jeremiah Gondwe," *Perspectives: Papers in the History, Politics and Economics of Africa Presented to Thomas Hodgkin*, ed. by C. Allen and R. W. Johnson. Cambridge: University Press.

Daneel, M. L.
   1971   *Old and New in Southern Shona Independent Churches, Vol. 1*. The Hague: Mouton.
   1974   *Old and New in Southern Shona Independent Churches, Vol. 2*. The Hague: Mouton.

Dillon-Malone
   1978   *The Korsten Basket Makers*. Manchester: Manchester University Press.

Hoole, M. C.
   n.d.   "The Historical Survey of Native Controlled Churches Operating in Nyasaland," Malawi National Archives, File 1A/1341.

Jules-Rosette, B.
   1975   *African Apostles*. Ithaca: Cornell University Press.

Livingstonia News
   1909-   Organ of the Free Church of Scotland Mission in
   1916   Malawi, (February 1909-October 1916).

Joseph C. Chakanza

Lohrentz, K.
   1971   "Joseph Booth, Charles Domingo and the Seventh-day
           Baptists in Northern Nyasaland," *Journal of African
           History*, 12(3).
Macdonald, R. J.
   1969   "Chronological List of Independent Churches in Malawi
           Till 1940," in *A History of African Education in Nyasa-
           land 1875-1945*, doctoral dissertation, Edinburgh.
   1970   "Religious Independency as a Means of Social
           Advancement in Northern Nyasaland in the 1930s,"
           Journal of Religion in Africa, 3(2).
Marwick, M. G.
   1950   "Another Modern Anti-witchcraft Movement in East
           Africa," *Africa*, 8(4).
McCracken, K. J.
   1977   *Politics and Christianity in Malawi 1875-1940*. London:
           Cambridge University Press.
Malawi National Archives
   1980- "History of Independent Churches," Malawi National
           Archives.
Mwasi, Yesaya Zerenji
   1933   "My Essential and Paramount Reasons for Working
           Independently," *Sources for the Study of Religion in
           Malawi*, no. 2. Department of Religious Studies, Univer-
           sity of Malawi.
Pachai, B.
   1972   "The State of the Churches in Malawi During the Early
           Protectorate Rule," *Journal of Social Sciences*,
           (Malawi), 1.
   1973   *Malawi: History of the Nation*. London: Longman.
Parratt, J. K.
   1978   "Y. Z. Mwasi and the Origins of the Blackman's
           Church," *Journal of Religion in Africa*, 3(2).
   1979   "Religious Independency in Nyasaland: A Typology of
           Origins," *African Studies*, 38(2).

Phiri, D. D.
1975-   *Great Malawians to Remember: Charles Chidongo*
1976   *Chinula* (1975), *John Chilembwe* (1976). Limbe: Long-
      man.
Ranger, Terence
1964   "Early History of Independency in Southern Rhodesia,"
      Religion in Africa, proceedings of a seminar held in the
      Centre of African Studies, University of Edinburgh, 10-
      12 April.
1971   "Christian Independency in Tanzania," *African Initia-
      tives in Religion*, ed. by D. B. Barrett. Nairobi: East
      African Publishing House.
1975   "The Mwana Lesa Movement of 1925," *Themes in the
      Christian History of Central Africa*. London: Heinemann.
Redmayne, Alison
1970   "Chikanga: An African Diviner with an International
      Reputation," *Witchcraft Confessions and Accusations*,
      ed. by M. Douglas. London: Tavistock Publications.
Richard, Audrey
1950   "A Modern Movement of Witch-finders," *Africa*, 8(4).
Shelburne, J. B.
1980   "Namikango Church Survey 1978-79," Churches of
      Christ Mission, Namikango, Zomba, 17 June.
Shepperson, G.
1954   "The Politics of an African Separatist Movement in
      British Central Africa, 1892-1916," *Africa*, 24(3).
Shepperson, G., and T. Price
1958   *Independent African: John Chilembwe and the Origins,
      Setting and Significance of the Nyasaland Native Rising of
      1915*. Edinburgh.
Sources for the Study of Religion in Malawi
1980   Department of Religious Studies, University of Malawi,
      nos. 2, 3, 8.
Sundkler, B.
1948-61 *Bantu Prophets in South Africa*. London: Oxford
      University Press for the International African Institute.
1976   *Zulu Zion*. London: Oxford University Press.

Joseph C. Chakanza

Turner, Harold W.
  1977   *Bibliography of New Religious Movements in Primal Soci-
          eties: Vol. 1, Black Africa.* Boston: G. K. Hall.
Wilson, Monica
  1959   *Communal Rituals of the Nyakyusa.* London: Oxford
          University Press for the International African Institute.
Wishlade
  1965   *Sectarianism in Southern Nyasaland.* London: Oxford
          University Press for the International African Institute.

Jack Thompson

Centre for New Religious Movements,
Selly Oak Colleges, Birmingham

An Independent church which never was: the case of Jonathan Chirwa

In the early years of the twentieth century the Christian history of northern Malawi was dominated by the Livingstonia Mission of the United Free Church of Scotland. While in many parts of Africa and even in other parts of Malawi ecclesiastical rivalry between the main Christian denominations was intense, in northern Malawi the Scots reigned supreme.

Yet in spite of, or perhaps because of, this ecclesiastical monopoly, between 1908 and 1933 a whole series of secessions led to the establishment of at least ten independent churches in a comparatively small area (Chakanza 1983). Since almost all of the new movements arising in northern Malawi in the period up to the 1930s would seem to fall at the independent church end of Harold Turner's typological spectrum, some new typology needs to be sought to distinguish the differences among them. John Parratt has attempted this in his "Religious Independency in Nyasaland: A Typology of Origins" (1979:183-200). While his three main groupings are useful in looking at new movements in Malawi as a whole, they are of limited value here, since his third group is made up of all secessions from the Livingstonia Mission. Nevertheless, his general approach of typologizing Malawi movements by their origins is helpful and can form the basis of a slightly more detailed typology for Livingstonia-derived movements themselves.

Jack Thompson

The question, What type of leaders formed new movements in the Livingstonia area? would appear to lead to the recognition of two main groups. The first group is made up of lay ex-members of the Livingstonia Mission who migrated outside the immediate Livingstonia area--sometimes as far as South Africa--where they came into contact with other movements, and returned to Malawi to begin their own movements in their home areas. Thus we could label this group the Lay External group. It would include Elliot Kamwana Chirwa (the Watchtower Bible and Tract Society, 1908); Charles Domingo (Seventh Day Baptists, 1910);[1] Jordan Msumba (Last Church of God and His Christ, 1925); the founders of the African National Church, 1927; I. C. Kaunda (Chipangano Church, 1927); and Paddy Nyasulu (the African Abraham Church, 1929).

The second major group is made up of ordained ministers of the Livingstonia Mission, who for various reasons began their own churches. By and large, there was no significant external theological influence involved. We could thus call this group the Ordained Internal group.

The churches begun by what I am calling the Ordained Internal group have been discussed widely elsewhere (McCracken 1977:273-85; Macdonald 1970:106-29; Parratt 1979:183-200; Parratt 1978:193-206; Thompson 1980:313-20), and it is not necessary to do more than list them here. They are the African Reformed Presbyterian Church founded by Rev. Yafet Mponda Mkandawire in 1932; the Blackman's Church of God which is in Tongaland, founded by Rev. Yesaya Zerenji Mwasi in 1933; and the Eklesia Lanangwa (Church of Freedom) founded by Rev. Charles Chidongo Chinula in 1934. Though the actual number of churches involved may thus appear to be small, they represent a considerable proportion of Livingstonia's theological graduates. Between 1914, when the first Livingstonia ministers were ordained, and 1925 a total of eleven ordinations took place. Of those eleven, six were to come under ecclesiastical discipline, and three were to begin their own independent churches.

A further significant question which immediately arises is, Were there any obvious theological, liturgical, or ecclesiological differences between the two groups? This is not our immediate concern here and would need further more detailed investigation. However, it may be noted in passing that, as might be expected, the churches

108

originating with the ordained Livingstonia ministers were, generally speaking, closely modeled on their Scottish parent, while those originating from lay initiatives displayed a greater variety of belief and practice.

The major purpose of this paper is to look in some detail at the case of Jonathan Chirwa, one of the early Livingstonia ministers who was suspended but who did not secede to form his own church. Since the issues involved in Chirwa's case were, in many respects, similar to those which produced the later secessions of Yafet Mkandawire, Y. Z. Mwasi, and Charles Chinula between 1932 and 1934, Chirwa was, we might say, the potential founder of an independent church. While he did not, in fact, secede, a study of his case may enable us to determine whether the later secessions might have been prevented.

Jonathan Chirwa had been one of the first three African ministers of the Livingstonia Mission, ordained on May 17, 1914. In the period immediately after his ordination he worked with the Scottish missionary Donald Fraser at Loudon (now Embangweni) and there began a friendship of unusual depth and mutual commitment. In 1916 Chirwa was transferred across the border to take charge of the mission station at Mwenzo in northeastern Zambia. While there he committed adultery, and following a confession to Fraser he resigned his ministry. At the Presbytery meeting of July 1918 he was suspended from church membership. Fraser himself recorded in the minutes, "With great sorrow the Presbytery heard their beloved brother Jonathan Chirwa make confession of sin and resign his ministry" (Livingstonia Minutes 1918).

Chirwa was the first Livingstonia minister to be suspended in this way, and there were no local precedents as to what should happen next. There was certainly a strong view held by some of the missionaries that any question of restoration to the ministry should be ruled out entirely, though no specific decision was taken at that time. For the next six years the dispute rumbled on. A major section of the African church, led by the Ngoni elders of the Loudon congregation and staunchly supported by Fraser, argued in favor of restoration, while a group of leading missionaries supported by a few African elders opposed restoration.

In July 1919 Presbytery received various petitions for the restoration of Jonathan Chirwa to the Christian ministry, and Fraser, together with Rev. Andrew Mkochi, reported on his conduct in the previous year. Presbytery decided by 23 votes to 9 that he should not be restored yet, but Mkochi and Fraser were given permission to appoint him to any work they saw fit (Livingstonia Minutes 1919).

That full restoration did not take place then, only twelve months after Chirwa's suspension, was hardly surprising, but when restoration was again refused the following year it became obvious that some members of Presbytery, including several influential missionaries, were opposed to restoration in the foreseeable future. The relevant minute recorded, "The fear was expressed by many speakers lest the Presbytery seem ahead of Christian public opinion and by a premature restoration lower the estimate of the Christian ministry at the very outset of its history in the country" (Livingstonia Minutes 1920). Yet it seems clear that, at least in uNgoni (the Mzimba district of modern Malawi where Chirwa came from and where he had carried out the early part of his ministry) public opinion favored restoration. An Ngoni elder of the period (now dead) was quite clear that "people wanted him to come back" (Mtonga 1971).

At this period in the history of the local church, the influence of the European missionaries in Presbytery was still great. Though numerically they were often outnumbered by more than three to one, their influence far outweighed their numbers. According to one local Christian, Chiswakhata Mkandawire (later to become one of the leading laymen in the church), "They tried to dominate" (Mkandawire 1977). Given this European domination of Presbytery, facilitated by the fact that many African elders were reluctant to vote against the wishes of their local European missionary, any hope of restoration for Chirwa depended upon a combination of local and missionary support. Between 1920 and 1923 Donald Fraser, who had consistently supported Chirwa, was on extended leave in Scotland, and in his absence no other European missionary seemed willing or able actively to pursue the case for restoration. In 1921 another petition for restoration from the Loudon group of congregations was presented by Andre Mkochi. The minutes merely record that as Jonathan Chirwa was not present no decision was taken (Livingstonia Minutes 1921). Those opposed to restoration were adopting the tactic of delay.

By now the divisions on the missionary side were becoming more clear-cut. At the beginning of 1921 Fraser had written from Scotland to W. A. Elmslie, one of the older Scottish missionaries who had worked among the Ngoni since 1885, protesting his dissatisfaction that Chirwa had not yet been restored and implying that such restoration would be in accordance with the mind of Christ (Fraser 1921). Elmslie dismissed such a view, claiming that "Paul's clear actions in an atmosphere such as we have point to caution." He went on to say, "I think Jonathan has been pampered since his case came up, and his repentance has made him a hero in the attitude of many. I myself think he should not have been permitted to take any public duties. He was suspended from the ministry which is not merely dispensing the sacraments" (Elmslie 1921). These latter references were to the fact that Chirwa, in accordance with the permission given to Fraser and Mkochi in 1919, had gradually been allowed to assume various ecclesiastical duties in the Loudon area and was by 1921 performing the duties of an evangelist (Moyo 1971).

In spite of missionary opposition, such as that of Elmslie, the Ngoni church continued with its efforts to have Chirwa restored. In July 1922 the Loudon session once again petitioned Presbytery for restoration. This time a special committee was set up to enquire into the case, and they reported back four days later that no final decision should be taken until the two European missionaries who had heard the original case had returned from furlough (Livingstonia Minutes 1922). This effectively postponed any decision until July 1924. But it also paved the way for a showdown then, for the two European missionaries involved were Fraser, who favored restoration, and Dr. Robert Laws, the leader of the mission for nearly 50 years, who was strongly opposed to it.

Following his return from furlough late in 1923, Fraser became once again directly involved in the case. Early in 1924 Fraser had gone on tour in the outlying areas of the Loudon district. He had taken Chirwa with him in order, among other things, to help dispense communion. In an article written about the trip Fraser had described Chirwa as "my beloved native helper" (Fraser 1924:264). It was clear that the time for a decision had arrived.

When Presbytery met in September 1924 at Livingstonia, the case was once again on the agenda. The Livingstonia Mission was on the

Jack Thompson

point of uniting with the Blantyre Mission of the Church of Scotland
to form the Church of Central Africa, Presbyterian. Those opposed
to restoration (including Dr. Laws and another of his missionary
allies, Rev. A. G. MacAlpine) now proposed that the case be
referred to a joint synod of Livingstonia and Blantyre. The Ngoni
church was by now in no mood for further delays, and two leading
Ngoni Christians, Andrew Mkochi and Yobe Nhlane, proposed "that
the case be proceeded with now" (Livingstonia Minutes 1924a). This
proposal was in itself a clear indication of their determination, for
seldom, if ever, up to that point had African Christians so directly
opposed the will of Laws. Their amendment to proceed with the case
was, nevertheless, carried by 29 votes to 5 (Livingstonia Minutes
1924a).

Immediately after that Mkochi moved and Fraser seconded "that
Jonathan Chirwa be now restored." Laws moved an amendment that
he be not restored. At this point the minutes merely record that the
meeting was adjourned for the night (Livingstonia Minutes 1924a),
but in fact the adjournment was necessary because the strong feelings being expressed on both sides were getting out of hand (Moyo
1971).

When the meeting was reconvened the following morning Laws
changed his amendment to "that Jonathan Chirwa be not restored
now" and was seconded by MacAlpine (Livingstonia Minutes
1924b). According to one eyewitness account, African opinion was
unanimously in favor of restoration, but Laws and MacAlpine
refused, arguing "it is not Law in Scotland" (Moyo 1971). Their
argument was that, for the purpose of maintaining the high moral
standards expected of the clergy, no minister guilty of a serious
moral lapse should ever be restored. This was a view which Fraser
had had to fight since 1918, for when the case had first come to light,
some had argued that he should be deposed with no hope of future
reinstatement. At the time Fraser had argued strongly against that
line, and now again in the Presbytery of 1924 and in answer to the
argument that it was not law in Scotland, he countered, "This is an
African church. We cannot take the laws of home" (Moyo 1971).

When a vote was eventually taken, only two voted not to restore
and 36 to restore, and Jonathan Chirwa was immediately reinstated
as a minister (Livingstonia Minutes 1924b). Four years later, in 1928,

112

he was elected Moderator of Presbytery, and he is remembered as one of the finest of the early Livingstonia ministers. By the early 1930s he had become an *éminence grise* at Loudon, described by one young missionary of the period as "a real father-in-God to me" and by another as "a very loving and loveable man" (Watson 1974; Taylor 1974).

Yet Jonathan Chirwa had had to wait over six years for restoration, amid growing discontent among those who supported him, and may certainly be regarded as the potential founder of an independent church. In many respects his case strongly resembles those of the three Livingstonia ministers who did later break away to form independent churches--Yaphet Mkandawire, Yesaya Zerenji Mwasi, and Charles Chinula. It remains to state briefly some of the common features of the cases of Chirwa and the three later secessionists, and finally to examine some of the reasons why Chirwa did not secede, in an attempt to determine whether the later secessions might have been prevented.

First of all, for those not familiar with them, here is a brief outline of the other three cases.[2] In 1932 Yafet Mkandawire was accused of taking *phemba*, a traditional medicine used to prevent one from being bewitched or poisoned. After investigation by Presbytery he was deposed from the Christian ministry and suspended from church membership, though about one third of Presbytery voted against deposition (Livingstonia Minutes 1932). Within a month Mkandawire had founded the African Reformed Presbyterian Church.

In the following year, the second of the three Ordained Internal secessions took place. Yesaya Zerenji Mwasi, one of the most brilliant academically of the early Livingstonia ministers, became involved in what began as a fairly simple dispute with his local elders at Sanga over a question of church discipline. The case was eventually referred to Presbytery--illegally in Mwasi's view. When Presbytery refused to support him, Mwasi announced his intention of resigning to form his own church, the Blackman's Church of God which is in Tongaland, which he did in 1933.

Meanwhile the third case had been proceeding longer. Charles Chinula had been ordained in 1925. In 1930 he was found guilty of adultery, deposed from his ministry, and suspended from church membership. He was restored to church membership in 1932, but by

Jack Thompson

1934 he had still not been reinstated as a minister. In July of that year he announced the formation of the Eklesia Lanangwa.

Though there were differences of detail, several immediate parallels among these three cases and that of Jonathan Chirwa come to mind. All four men were involved in lengthy disputes with Presbytery. Though Mkandawire's case appears to be brief, it was, in fact, the culmination of several disputes (Parratt 1970:198). In three of the four cases--Mwasi being the exception--the dispute led to suspension. In all four cases there was considerable local support for the men involved, as witnessed both by the debates in Presbytery and--in the case of the three seceders--by the following they quickly gathered in their new churches. Finally, a careful study of the cases reveals an underlying racial tension manifested in the differing approaches to discipline of the more legalistic of the missionaries on the one hand and many local Christians on the other.

In view of these similarities (in a longer study others could be cited) the question might be asked, Why did Jonathan Chirwa not secede as his three colleagues did later? Put another way the question might be, What were the essential differences between Chirwa's case and those of the other three?

To begin with, Chirwa's was the first such case, and the lack of a precedent gave hope of restoration, which was eventually realized. It might be thought that once this precedent was established it would have been an incentive to those who came later to remain in the church and wait for restoration. Here, however, the question of personality cannot be ignored. Chirwa was a quiet, gentle, patient man, not given to sudden outbursts or confrontation. The other three (especially Mwasi and Chinula) were different. Both Mwasi and Chinula were well known for their outspokenness in Presbytery and other places and were involved in the beginnings of the proto-nationalist movement in Malawi. ("Sit down Mwasi. You are going to be arrested," one of his more timid colleagues had advised after one clash with the missionaries in Presbytery, to which Mwasi replied, "No I will not sit down. This is the church" (Mkandawire 1977).) By contrast, the same informant described Jonathan Chirwa's attitude towards the missionaries as *nthena-nthena*, i.e. so-so, balancing (Mkandawire 1977).

114

Of crucial importance in Chirwa's case was the joint support of the local church and the missionary Donald Fraser. As pointed out earlier, missionary power in Presbytery was out of all proportion to numbers, and Fraser's support for Chirwa was constant and unflinching, eventually winning over all of his colleagues except Laws and MacAlpine. Such support encouraged local Christians to make their views known, and this, together with the evident repentance of Chirwa, was enough to carry the day. No such concerted support was evident in any of the later cases. Though local support was considerable, it had to contend with a hardening of missionary attitudes in the 1930s.

Changes in missionary personnel during this period should not be ignored. In the 1920s many of the pioneer missionaries, with careers dating back to before the turn of the century, were still working. Men like Laws, Elmslie, MacAlpine, and Fraser were viewed with varying combinations of affection, respect, awe, and fear. By the early 1930s all of these had gone--MacAlpine was at the point of retiring when Y. Z. Mwasi's case occurred. They had been replaced by younger missionaries who were the contemporaries, or even the juniors, of many of the African clergy. These clergy were in turn becoming more self-confident and assertive. When disputes did blow up, men like Mwasi and Chinula were not prepared to submit to this new generation of missionary in the same way that they had to the old.

Yet for all these differences one cannot avoid feeling that the lessons of Jonathan Chirwa's case were not learned in the late 1920s and early 1930s. The churches formed by Mkandawire, Mwasi, and Chinula were caused not by a prophetic vision but by a breakdown in relationships. On this level at least they might be said to have been avoidable.

What then were the lessons which might have been learned as a result of Chirwa's case? First is a wider recognition by the missionaries of the cultural strains imposed on the early African ministers by what was basically a foreign system of values. Such a recognition might have enabled a more flexible approach in cases like Mkandawire's. Second is the provision of more sympathetic pastoral care in those cases where suspension was still thought to be necessary. It is possible that the pastoral care provided by Andrew Mkochi and

Donald Fraser was the most important single factor in preventing Chirwa's secession. Third is the need to prevent missionary/African polarization in extreme cases in Presbytery. This polarization was often masked by the tendency of some African elders to vote with their missionary but was nevertheless a real issue.[3] Finally, a determined effort to discover and trust the views of the African church on such matters might well have produced more positive results.

This is not to argue that the churches founded by Mkandawire, Mwasi, and Chinula--which united as the Blackman's Church in 1935--were entirely negative or regrettable developments. To begin with, they provided a place for those who might otherwise have been outside Christian structures. The fact that the Blackman's Church continues to exist is some indication of this. In addition, Charles Chinula, a noted hymn-writer, produced some of his most powerful compositions during this period of trauma (Phiri 1975:22-26; Kaunda 1971-73), and Y. Z. Mwasi's written justification for his secession, "My Essential and Paramount Reasons for Working Independently," is an important historical statement of the underlying tensions between missionaries and African leaders which would not have emerged otherwise (Mwasi 1979).

Nevertheless, the Ordained Internal group of secessions was brought about by tensions and disagreements within the Livingstonia set-up rather than by any new or startling theological insights. The talents of the three men concerned might have been better used within the Church of Central Africa, Presbyterian. In this sense, at least, the secessions were regrettable. Had the lessons of Chirwa's case been better learned, and had the cases of Mkandawire, Mwasi, and Chinula been handled with more sensitivity, then it is at least possible that each of them, like Jonathan Chirwa, would have been the founder of an independent church which never was.

NOTES

1. To some extent Charles Domingo straddles both groups, since, although he was not formally ordained, he had completed the Livingstonia theological course in 1900 and was licensed as a Probationer in 1902, although not ordained before leaving the mission in 1908.

2.   For more details of these cases, see McCracken 1977:273-85; Macdonald 1970:106-29; Parratt 1979:183-200; Parratt 1978:193-206; Thompson 1980:313-20.

3.   Almost all my local informants, once I got to know them, made this point with some force.

REFERENCES
Chakanza, J. C.
      1983   "An Annotated List of Independent Churches in
                Malawi," *Sources for the Study of Religion in Malawi*,
                No. 10 (2nd revised edition).
Fraser, Donald
      1921   Quoted in Elmslie to Laws, 28 January 1921, Livingstonia
                Papers, Box 9, National Archives of Malawi 1924, article
                in Monthly Record of the United Free Church of Scot-
                land, June.
Elmslie, W. A.
      1921   Quoted in Elmslie to Laws, 28 January 1921, Livingstonia
                Papers, Box 9, National Archives of Malawi.
Kaunda, Y. C., Rev.
      1971-   Various informal conversations.
      1973
Livingstonia Minutes
      1918   Livingstonia Presbytery Minutes, 22 July 1918, National
                Archives of Malawi.
      1919   Livingstonia Minutes, 23 July 1919.
      1920   Livingstonia Minutes, 20 July 1920.
      1921   Livingstonia Minutes, 25 July 1921.
      1922   Livingstonia Minutes, 20 and 24 July 1922.
      1924a   Livingstonia Minutes, 11 September 1924.
      1924b   Livingstonia Minutes, 12 September 1924.
      1932   Livingstonia Minutes, 22 October 1932.
Macdonald, R. J.
      1970   "Religious Independency as a Means of Social
                Advancement in Northern Nyasaland in the 1930's,"
                Journal of Religion in Africa, 3(2).

McCracken, John
  1977   *Politics and Christianity in Malawi, 1875-1940.*
          Cambridge.
Mkandawire, William Chriswakhata
  1977   Personal interview, 21 January.
Moyo, Petros H.
  1971   Personal interview, 28 December.
Mtongo, Muwalo, Rev.
  1971   Personal interview, 29 December.
Mwasi, Y. Z.
  1979   "My Essential and Paramount Reasons for Working
          Independently," *Sources for the Study of Religion in
          Malawi*, No. 2, Zomba (originally 1933).
Parratt, J. K.
  1978   "Y. Z. Mwasi and the Origins of the Blackman's
          Church," *Journal of Religion in Africa*, 9:(3).
  1979   "Religious Independency in Nyasaland--A Typology of
          Origins," *African Studies* (Johannesburg), 38(2).
Phiri, D. D.
  1975   *Malawians to Remember: Charles Chidongo Chinula.*
          Lilongwe, Malawi.
Taylor, Helen M.
  1974   Personal interview, 16 January.
Thompson, T. J.
  1980   "Fraser and the Ngoni," unpublished Ph.D. thesis.
          University of Edinburgh.
Watson, W. H.
  1974   Personal communication, 8 October.

John Parratt
University of Botswana

The Malikebu case

The early history of the Providence Industrial Mission (PIM) is well known from the career of the Rev. John Chilembwe, the leader of the first movement to assert independence in colonial Nyasaland and the country's first political martyr (Shepperson and Price 1958). Less well known is the subsequent story of the PIM from its reopening in 1926 under Chilembwe's successor, the Rev. Dr. Daniel Sharpe Malikebu, up until his death in 1978. In this paper I shall look briefly at Malikebu's career before examining in more detail the unhappy events which saddened the final years of this gifted and dedicated man.[1]

Daniel Malikebu was born in the early 1890s in the Chiradzulu District of southern Nyasaland.[2] He attended the PIM school and was baptized as one of Chilembwe's first converts. Subsequently he became a house servant of Miss Emma DeLany (Shepperson and Price 1958:132ff., 142ff.), one of the black American missionaries of the National Baptist Convention's Foreign Mission Board (FMB) who had been sent to support Chilembwe's work. After Miss DeLany returned home in June 1906 her young protegé followed her, making his way on foot to the coast[3] and then working his passage to America. He spent a decade there, completing a course in theology at the Moody Bible Institute and subsequently obtaining his M.D. at the Meharry Medical College in Nashville.[4] Shortly afterwards he married Flora Ethelwyn, who had been born in the Congo Free State and taken to America as a baby.

The Malikebus visited Nyasaland briefly in 1921, but it would appear that at that time the trauma of the 1915 Rising was still too fresh in the memory of the colonial government to permit the reopening of the PIM. By 1926, however, the climate of opinion had changed. The Malikebus returned to Nyasaland in February of that year, and after some correspondence between the FMB and the government, they were permitted to reopen the mission. Malikebu, who had in any case been out of the country during the Chilembwe Rising, was judged politically harmless, and he was also under strict instructions from the FMB to avoid any political involvement.[5] Under Malikebu's leadership progress appears to have been rapid. By the end of 1926 a school had been established, which was soon receiving a grant-in-aid from the education department of the colonial government (Macdonald 1975:222ff.) In the following year Malikebu was registered on the medical sub-register as a hospital assistant (MNA IA/1341). By the time the Malikebus returned to the United States in 1938 for a long-delayed furlough, the PIM had been fully reestablished.[6]

They came back to Nyasaland in 1945. Soon after this the PIM was incorporated under the Trustees Incorporation Ordinance as the National Baptist Assembly, Inc.--presumably to bring its name more in line with that of the parent body. But the name PIM continued to be used, and Dr. Malikebu was designated as chairman of both bodies (Civil Cause 319:8). During the early 1960s, however, administrative problems began to show up. On the one hand, the education department became concerned over the nonpayment of the mission's teachers for which the grant-in-aid had been given. As no satisfactory account of this state of affairs was forthcoming, the PIM's school was closed by government order (Civil Cause 319:9) not to reopen until 1971. At the same time, the FMB of the National Baptist Convention became involved. Its practice had been to pay the stipends of several of the PIM ministers and other church workers, as well as funding certain mission projects. As it happened, the ministers concerned had not been paid regularly, nor had the funded projects been carried out. Neither Malikebu, as chairman, nor the minister in charge of finances was able to give a satisfactory explanation (Civil Cause 319:9-10).[7] At the beginning of 1971 the FMB sent a delegate to Malawi,[8] Dr. William Harvey III, to investigate the tangled finances of the PIM. Harvey uncovered evidence of mismanagement and embezzlement. He made a number of recommendations, including the dismissal of certain officers responsible for the mission funds. He also directed that Dr. Malikebu's personal bank account should be kept clearly separate from that of the PIM (Civil Cause 319:10).[9] On his return to America Harvey reported the problems to the FMB and was given wide discretionary powers to deal with the situation as he felt fit. It is perhaps significant that in February of the same year the Registrar-General received two requests from the PIM, which changed its name to the "African Baptist Assembly (Malawi) Inc.," thus effectively removing the similarity of name between the PIM and the American body. Malikebu remained as chairman, and the trustees included the Rev. J. J. Mang'anda and Rev. B. B. Nadolo, whom we shall meet again below (Civil Cause 319:15-16).[10] In other respects too the relationship between the Malawian and American bodies was showing signs of strain. Early in 1971 one of the FMB's missionaries at Chiradzulu, Miss Josephine Mintor, had been deported from the country for contravening the somewhat strict dress regulations imposed upon females after independence.[11] It was later alleged that Miss Mintor had been reported to the police by Rev. Nadolo.[12]

Harvey came back to Malawi in August 1971 to carry into effect his mandate to deal with the abuses of management in the PIM. His visit was timed to coincide with the annual convention of the African Baptist Assembly (Malawi) Inc., which attracted delegates from several neighboring countries. In the six months since his previous visit, the PIM's finances had continued to deteriorate; ministers' salaries remained unpaid, debts for which funds had been provided for by the FMB were still outstanding, and creditors were pressing for payment. American funds were clearly being misused and mismanaged. Dr. Harvey seems to have determined on a preemptive strike to disarm possible opposition from the older PIM ministers. On August 9, the day before the mission's assembly, he convened a meeting of some of the church's leaders, including Dr. Malikebu, at the Mount Soche, Blantyre's largest hotel. Neither Rev. Mang'anda nor Rev. Nadolo, First and Second Vice-Chairman respectively, seem to have been invited. At Harvey's suggestion this informal meeting passed several resolutions. Rev. Nadolo, Miss Mintor's accuser, was to be defrocked; the same sentence was meted out to the Rev. Mdala, who had been responsible for PIM's fund problems. In his case, a summary "internal deportation order" was served that he should remove himself from the mission headquarters within 48 hours. Dr. Malikebu himself, in view of his advanced age and the ill health of his wife, was to be retired to the United States on a pension provided by the FMB. Malikebu apparently concurred in all these decisions. Having thus prepared the ground for the annual meeting, the company broke up.

The official convention took place at the Mbombwe, Chiradzulu, headquarters the next day. According to the High Court judgment, Harvey briefed Malikebu before the meeting that the Rev. L. C. Muocha should be proposed as Malikebu's successor as chairman (Civil Cause 319:11). Muocha was a younger minister of the PIM, having been ordained in 1949. He was previously Malikebu's domestic servant and married one of his nieces. Muocha served the church in several different countries and on occasions looked after Malikebu's house during his absences. More important, he had at times acted as chairman, in which capacity he had sent reports to the FMB in America.

The annual meeting itself went according to plan. Dr. Malikebu introduced Harvey as an emissary of the FMB of the National Baptist Convention, and the latter then advised the meeting of the decision to retire Malikebu and to take him and his wife to the United States on a pension. This proposal was unanimously approved (Civil Cause 319:12).[13] The Malikebus were to remain for a month in Malawi to wind up their affairs. Harvey then told the meeting that, with Malikebu's approval, he had appointed Rev. Muocha as chairman. This too, apparently, received overwhelming support. Having successfully accomplished this coup d'église, Harvey departed from Malawi. Malikebu himself did not leave until November 12. Before he left, he called a meeting in Chiradzulu, to which the local M.P. and representatives of the police and the Malawi Congress Party were invited, where he publicly announced his retirement and confirmed Muocha as chairman.

It soon became clear that Harvey's exclusion of the older ministers from the corridors of ecclesiastical power was not wholly successful. The two former vice-chairmen, Rev. Mang'anda and Rev. Nadolo, made no secret of their disaffection that Malikebu had been succeeded by someone far below them in the PIM hierarchy. Muocha, for his part, wisely summoned a meeting at Chiradzulu at which it was denied there was a schism in the church, and

Mang'anda subsequently wrote to Muocha confirming his loyalty (Civil Cause 319:14).[14] It soon became obvious that this was far from the case. An open split developed between the two parties, leading to police intervention in conflicts over the possession of churches in Limbe, Thyolo, and Balaka. Rev. Nadolo--who was dismissed over the incident of Miss Mintor's allegedly truncated skirts--finding himself excluded from the PIM's churches, started to conduct services for his followers in a shed on the outskirts of Limbe. The point at issue now became clear: Mang'anda, Nadolo, and others disputed the legality of the retirement of Dr. Malikebu, asserting that he was still the rightful chairman of PIM. To complicate matters, Mang'anda, because of his former position as corresponding secretary, had gained possession of the certificate of incorporation and of the common seal and refused to surrender them to Muocha. The latter's attempt to register his own list of trustees therefore could not be accepted by the Registrar-General. Muocha's supporters, for their part, retained possession of most of the PIM property, including the Chiradzulu headquarters. By this time, Malikebu himself had substantially modified his own position, no doubt in response to appeals from the Mang'anda party. By 1975 he was writing to Malawi claiming that he had never been retired and was still the chairman of the PIM. He appealed to the police in Chiradzulu to eject Muocha who, he claimed, had occupied his home without authority. In June of that year he sent a letter to the Regional Minister for the South, claiming that the church had been built by self-help and with the agreement of the village headman, and that agents of the FMB had gained possession of the mission under false pretences.[15] There was an abortive attempt by the Malawi Congress Party to solve the dispute before it moved to its inevitable conclusion. The registered trustees of the African Baptist Assembly (Malawi) Inc. (i.e., Mang'anda's group) brought a case against Rev. Muocha over his use of PIM's name and property. Both Dr. Malikebu and Dr. Harvey returned to Malawi to give evidence[16] when the case was heard in the High Court, Blantyre, in 1977.

The case was a protracted one, and judgment was not given until September 6, 1978. It was, as Mr. Justice Chatsika remarked in the course of his masterly summing up, "a case rich with the early history of the Providence Industrial Mission in Malawi [and] clearly

John Parratt

marked with overtones and undertones of a political nature" (Civil Cause 319:3). Its outcome rested on two interrelated issues: did Dr. Harvey have the authority to retire Dr. Malikebu, and did he have the right to appoint Rev. Muocha in his place? In other words, was the PIM an independent mission, or was it under the control of the FMB of the National Baptist Convention?

The Court found in favor of the FMB on both issues. It took evidence that in 1924 Malikebu had applied to the FMB for employment as a missionary and had been given letters of credence from that body. There was also undisputed evidence that the FMB had financed projects of the PIM. Furthermore, during his furlough Malikebu had been appointed supervisor of the FMB's missions in Zambia and South Africa, an appointment he had accepted. It was therefore "a fact that Dr. Malikebu was employed by the FMB" (Civil Cause 319:18-19; MNA 1A/1341). It was also found that he had knowingly accepted regular pension payments from the Board. He had therefore been properly retired. The question of Muocha's appointment turned also upon another factor, namely, that of the ownership of the PIM property. Evidence was produced in court that Chilembwe, prior to his return to Nyasaland in 1900, had appealed to the National Baptist Convention for funds and that for technical reasons he had sold the rights of the mission land to the FMB. Muocha therefore had been legally appointed by Dr. Harvey on behalf of the proprietors of the mission.

In pronouncing judgment, Mr. Justice Chatsika nevertheless expressed his concern that Dr. Harvey had acted "rather high-handedly and that consequently people such as Rev. Mang'anda felt they had been slighted" (Civil Cause 319:19). And certainly the FMB's representative had shown an extraordinary insensitiveness to the feelings of the ministers who were in positions of authority and a very un-African lack of respect for the church's gerontocracy.[17] The FMB comes out of the affair with more than a taint of ecclesiastical colonialism.

But what of Malikebu himself? Three criticisms of his character have been advanced from his actions. The first is the charge that he was authoritarian and that he deliberately, up until his forcible retirement, kept all the control of the church in his own hands. As far as one can see, only one of the ministers was sent to America for training during the whole period, 1926-1971. Malikebu in fact had no ministers remotely rivaling him in educational attainments. Mang'anda, who described himself as having been taken in as a boy by Malikebu and received all his education at Malikebu's hands, was an articulate but not highly trained vice-chairman. A second aspect to the charge of authoritarianism is the fact that there were several secessions from the PIM during Malikebu's leadership. The earliest of these was the Achewa Providence Industrial Mission of Peter Kaluba (MNA 1A/1341; Chakanza 1983:3; see also note 7). Further secessions appeared from 1946 onward, and significantly one of these was led by Rev. Saviya, the only PIM minister known to have been trained in the United States (Chakanza 1983:56-57). Since these secessions do not, on the whole, seem to have been over matters of doctrine[18] we must probably assume that they were primarily conflict over leadership. The charge of authoritarianism may thus have some basis.

Second, there is the question of financial mismanagement. There is obvious evidence of serious abuse of the PIM funds, for which the ultimate responsibility must rest with Malikebu as chairman. I can find no evidence, however, that he himself was ever accused of appropriating funds for his own gain (see note 7). The fault seems to have been rather one of lack of oversight and of misjudgment of the character of some of those whom he employed.

Finally, there is the charge that Malikebu was inconsistent and vacillating after he had accepted the decision of the FMB to retire him. Of this there can be no doubt, for his letters from America denying his retirement were indeed an extraordinary volte face. Possibly he felt he had been deceived by Harvey into disclaiming his position as chairman and found that the emotional bond with the mission which he had raised up from nothing and nourished for most of his life was too strong to be so quickly severed. But perhaps again--and there is some evidence of this--his actions should not be seen as the perversities of a capricious nature but as part of the sad decline in his faculties brought about by his advanced age.

Whatever the truth or otherwise of these supposed shortcomings of character, they seem to me insignificant in comparison with his remarkable achievements and his pioneering contribution to indigenous Christianity in Malawi. In the same month the High Court judgment was given, Dr. Daniel Malikebu withdrew to found a new church.[19] He was a saddened man of nearly 90, alienated from the mission he had spent half a century serving as medical doctor, educator, and minister of religion. A few weeks later he was dead. He was buried on October 10, 1978, at his home village in Chiradzulu. There was no obituary for him in the national press.

NOTES

1. Besides published and unpublished sources cited below, I wish to acknowledge my indebtedness to the following for information concerning Dr. Malikebu: Rev. J. J. Mang'anda (oral testimonies in 1978, 1979--appropriately taken together with Harold Turner--and in 1980 by students in the Department of Religious Studies, University of Malawi; the Very Rev. J. Sangaya (personal communication, 1978); Rev. L. C. Muocha (personal communication, 1984); and various members of the Malikebu family (personal communications, 1984). I am especially grateful to Mr. L. A. Chatsika, formerly Justice of the High Court of Malawi and currently Dean of the Faculty of Law and Public Administration, University of Malawi, with whom I have had several conversations about the court case.

2. For Malikebu's early years, see further Shepperson and Price (1958:142ff.), John Parratt (*African Studies* 38/2:183ff.), and especially the full account of R. J. Macdonald (1975:215-33). Important unpublished sources held in the Malawi National Archives include MNA file IA/1341 (1940).

3. According to Shepperson and Price (1958:142), Cape Town; according to Macdonald (1975), Beira. The latter seems more probable and was confirmed by Mang'anda.

4. The parallels with President H. K. Banda are many and striking. There is no evidence, however, that Malikebu ever involved himself in politics, either before or after independence (Macdonald 1975:233).

5. See the letter from J. E. East, corresponding secretary of the FMB, dated Dec. 21, 1926, in which he warns Malikebu not to appear politically dangerous by employing those of suspect loyalty, and "under no circumstances to tolerate any political or seditious

speaking in the mission station." The letter is quoted in MNA IA/1341.

6. According to MNA 1A/1341 he left with the intention of raising money for the mission and stated that he would not return if he failed to do so. According to Mang'anda, Malikebu possessed an American passport.

7. There was a further matter of a quantity of second-hand clothes, donated by the FMB for free distribution, but which were found for sale in PIM's shop. According to MNA 1A/1341, Dr. Malikebu had come under the suspicion of some of the PIM members as early as 1937 for his fundraising activities which culminated in the purchase of a Chevrolet lorry. It is not clear whether the timing of the furlough was connected with these events. As indicated in note 6, one reason for his departure was to raise funds for the PIM, and this seems to be confirmed by Macdonald (1975:229-30). In the latter's view, however, the main reason for the furlough was the ill health of Mrs. Malikebu. It seems likely that the first secession from the PIM, that of the Achewa Providence Mission, occurred at this time. The reason for the split may have been connected with the financial problems. It is unlikely that it was purely tribal since the PIM does not seem to have used the epithet "Ajawa" (i.e. Yao) at all during Malikebu's time; in fact Malikebu himself was a Mang'anja, a sub-group of the Chewa (Chakanza 1983:3).

8. On July 6, 1964, Nyasaland became the independent state of Malawi.

9. His recommendation that more than one signatory should be required for the PIM account implies that Malikebu had previously had total discretion in the use of funds, though there was no suggestion of dishonesty on his part. According to MNA IA/1341 Malikebu had received funds from the FMB through the Standard Bank.

10. The popular name "PIM" continued to be used. According to Chakanza (1983:7) the new name "African Baptist Assembly" was introduced in 1973; presumably this refers to a subsequent reregistration.

11. Ostensibly in the interests of traditional custom Malawi law requires women to wear skirts which cover the knee; this was more strictly enforced in the 1970s.

12. Civil Cause 319 (p. 11) indicates that the subsequent meeting at the Mount Soche hotel considered Nadolo's allegations as false. Oral testimony at present available to me does not demonstrate whether Nadolo's motive was antagonism to the FMB missionary or whether it sprang from a genuine desire to maintain the standards of legal Malawian female decency in the church.

13. I can find no confirmation of Mang'anda's claim that an altercation broke out at this point or that Malikebu asserted that he "had not been employed by anybody," since his work was a divine call. This seems to reflect his attitude of some years later.

14. The letter was produced in Court.

15. The letters, now in Mang'anda's possession, were sent from Spellman College, Mrs. Malikebu's alma mater, which had also from time to time supported the PIM financially (see MNA 1A/1341). The claim to self-help was indeed true (Macdonald 1975:222, 227) though, as we shall see below, the question of ownership was more complicated.

16. There is evidence that Malikebu's entrance into Malawi was delayed for technical reasons. He was not permitted to stay in Chiradzulu or in Blantyre or to preach or canvass his case. He stayed at Mulanje, at what later became the headquarters of the Independent Baptist Convention.

17. The practice of "fixing" decisions of church bodies by a strategic preliminary meeting of the missionaries and their supporters, which excluded possible opponents, was a ploy which seems to have been perfected in the 1920s and 1930s by the Livingstonia missionaries and was one factor in the secessions in the north during this period.

18. Chakanza points out that Saviya was a former Catholic, and his church adopted some Catholic practices.

19. The new church was the Independent Baptist Convention. According to Mang'anda, half of the 40 PIM ministers seceded with Malikebu.

REFERENCES

Chakanza, J. C.
1983   "An Annotated List of Independent Churches in Malawi," *Sources for the Study of Religion in Malawi*, no. 10, Zomba.

Civil Cause 319
1977   High Court of Malawi (Blantyre) Civil Cause No. 319 of 1977, Judgment by Mr. Justice Chatsika.

East, J. E.
1926   Letter dated Dec. 21, 1926, quoted in MNA 1A/1341.

Macdonald, R. J.
1975   "Rev. Daniel Sharpe Malikebu and the Reopening of the Providence Industrial Mission: 1926-39," *From Nyasaland to Malawi*, ed. by R. J. Macdonald. Nairobi.

Malawi National Archives
1940   *A Historical Survey of Native Controlled Missions Operating in Nyasaland*. MNA file 1A/1341.

Parratt, John
n.d.   "Religious Independency in Nyasaland, A Typology of Origins," *African Studies* 38(2).

Shepperson, G., and T. Price
1958   *Independent African: John Chilembwe and the Origins, Setting and Significance of the Nyasaland Native Rising of 1915*. Edinburgh.

John Parratt

Rosalind I. J. Hackett
University of Tennessee

Enigma variations: the new religious movement in Nigeria today

"Not being able to see the wood for the trees" is the expression which comes to mind when one reflects on the myriad new religious movements in Nigeria today. If one is wise, one turns to Harold Turner's invaluable work on the classification and description of African New Religious Movements. His typologies have served as a reassuring yardstick and guiding light for those of us who have been involved in the teaching and researching of new religious movements (Turner 1979a:49-62; 1979b:79-108).

But as Harold Turner knows almost better than anyone else, the processes of deforestation and reforestation are significant features of the Nigerian religious landscape. My intention here is to highlight some of the changes I encountered in the course of field work on new religious movements in Nigeria from 1975-1983--notably in the southeastern town of Calabar--and discuss their implications for definition and classification.

Just as the independent church has come to epitomize the new religious movement in Africa today, the Aladura or prophet-healing church is seen as the standard model in terms of religious innovation and independency in Nigeria. This is attributable to sheer size--at least one in four Christians in Nigeria claims adherence to this type of church--and to the vast amount of documentation which exists on these movements. Some documentation has been produced by the movements themselves, but the main bulk of the literature stems from academics and other outside observers who see the Aladura churches as important examples of cultural and religious synthesis and innovation in response to social and religious change.

Rosalind I. J. Hackett

Yet the image of the independent church as something fiercely autonomous, ostensibly African, and primarily indigenous is being increasingly undermined by the emergence of new religious movements which we have chosen to label as revivalist movements and spiritual science movements.

The revivalist movement

The Truth and Life Ministries International (TLMI) is a good example of the revivalist movement. Islamic-related movements with fundamentalist leanings may also be included in this category, but we are limiting our examples here to Christian-related movements since these predominated in our field of research. The revivalist movement origins follow the pattern of emergence of many independent churches: it developed from a small prayer group within the Apostolic Church, a British-related Pentecostal church in Calabar in the late 1970s. Outwardly it does not resemble the typical image of an African independent church, for it lacks the ritual symbolism, taboos, and music normally associated with such churches. It seems to owe more to nonindigenous origins and influences than to its own indigenous roots. This is particularly evident in the language and doctrines which are distinctly Pentecostal and evangelical. Preaching styles recall those of the American born-again evangelist rather than the African prophet. Music is gospel-style and played on electronic instruments; the male choristers wear bow ties and the women long black skirts and white blouses.

The aims of the TLMI are enshrined on their new bus:

CHURCH PLANTING EVANGELISM DELIVERANCE
BIBLE STUDIES

The founder, Rev. Dr. A. O. Akwaowo, an Ibibio man in his forties, emphasizes the importance of the more pluralistic and embracing concept of ministries rather than the more restrictive notion of a church. The historical development of TLMI can be traced as follows:

Truth and Life Evangelistic Group	1977
Truth and Life Church	1979
Construction of church building	1980
Truth and Life Church International	1981
Truth and Life Ministries International	1982

Interestingly enough, TLMI during the middle span of its existence opted for the church model, but more recently has sought a wider orientation with a radio, television, and cassette ministry, as well as a monthly newsletter and magazine (*The Miracles*). The "Deliverance Hour Ministry" publishes the transcripts of the sermons of Akwaowo, which treat such topics as "The New Birth," "The Rapture and the Second Coming of Christ," and "Have Faith in God." There is also a business reply service and mailing list which allows nonmembers to benefit from the ministry.

The use of such techniques stems largely from the business acumen and dynamism of the founder, formerly a Personal Secretary in the state government. His organizational skills have also been strongly influenced by his American training and experience; he attended a three-month Bible conference in San Diego and received an Honorary Doctorate of Divinity from a seminary in Rossville, Georgia.

TLMI, which now has over 400 baptized members--in three branches on the mainland part of the Cross River State in addition to the headquarters in Calabar--and scores of nonmember supporters, exhibits a remarkable degree of what may be termed internationalism. We understand internationalism to be the establishing of, or desire to establish, international contacts in the religious field. TLMI has built up a considerable network of international relationships: the Osborn Foundation International (Tulsa, Oklahoma); Christ for the Nations, Inc. (USA); Oral Roberts Evangelistic Association (Tulsa, Oklahoma); Covington Theological Seminary (Georgia); Church of God Mission International (Benin City); Scripture Gift Mission (London); Faith Pool Prayer Groups (Ghana and Florida). The relationship of TLMI with these groups is not one of dependency; it is rather one of spiritual counseling and supplementation through the provision of books, tracts, cassette tapes, and perhaps the occasional visit of a representative. Some financial aid was received from the All Nations For Christ Program (Texas) to help establish a branch at Itu. Rev. Akwaowo believes firmly in the importance of spiritual independence for his organization and its followers. He has plans to establish a printing press and Bible school. He is responsible for the founding of an international evangelistic team whose members (from Nigeria, United States, United

Kingdom, and India) evangelize in one another's countries. The various representatives all met during a Bible conference in the U.S. in 1981. To this end, Akwaowo undertook a missionary journey to India (Kotagiri, Coimbatore, Singanallur) in March 1983 (*The Miracles* 1983:3-4). Within Nigeria itself, Akwaowo has adopted a cooperative attitude towards other churches and evangelistic associations. He was chairman of the interdenominational committee for the International Year of the Disabled and encourages freelance preachers, including women, to use his pulpit. He is wary, however, of merger or affiliation attempts.

For any religious organization to succeed in Nigeria, its worldview must correspond at some point with those of its potential adherents, and it must offer a blueprint for action in accordance with people's needs. In this respect the TLMI does not differ from any other religious group which is enjoying sustained growth and development. Healing, prayer, and miracles are vital components of the world of TLMI. For those unable to come to the compound for prayer and laying on of hands, "faith-prayer cloths" are sent to them or they are visited at home. For those troubled by witchcraft, fasting and prayer are the prescriptions for deliverance. In place of ritualistic techniques, the supplicant is treated to soteriological concepts and evangelical rhetoric mediated and interpreted by Akwaowo and his team for local needs. Akwaowo does not, therefore, represent the charismatic figure as characterized by many independent African church leaders; he is rather the leader with rational-legal authority who uses his entrepreneurial skills to organize a small, yet rapidly growing ecclesiastical business.

The organization created by Akwaowo is not an isolated example of this new breed of independent church.[1] It is new in that these groups, while founded by Nigerians for Nigerians (and others) in Nigeria (and beyond), are drawing increasingly on a repertoire of language and techniques, forms and concepts, which stems largely from the American evangelical and Pentecostal traditions and which determines their character and orientation. Other examples of this new breed of religious movement within Calabar are the Revival Valley Ministries, the Christ Life Evangelistic Ministry, the Deeper Christian Life Ministry, Akrasi Evangelism, Jesus Christ Healing and Evangelical Movement, the New Testament Ministry, and the

Missionary Fellowship. One of the largest such movements in Nigeria is the God Mission International in Benin City, founded by Rev. B. Idahosa who is well known as an affluent "show-biz crusader." The organization owns a well-equipped television studio, a 30,000 capacity cathedrome, and a post-primary school known as the Word of Faith Day School (*Concord Weekly* 1985:9).

As their self-designation suggests, these organizations see their role as supplementary to that of the churches; they want a wider, nondenominational clientele. Such inclusivist tendencies have not been a predominant feature of the mission or later sectarian churches in the area. The revivalist movements are characterized by an internationalist and expansionist vision; they are motivated by a new identity (as "born again" and sanctified Christians) and a redefined concept of salvation (more personally and theologically oriented). They are characterized by more flexible structures than the conventional church model, i.e., if they hold regular worship it is generally less important than other activities such as crusades, postal religion, broadcasting and literature evangelism, conventions, and camp meetings.

The spiritual science movement

The spiritual science movement is even further removed from the independent church model since it promotes alternative structures and its content is in no way Christian-related. This type of movement defies easy definition because of its heterogeneity--occultism, metaphysics, mysticism, and the magical and psychic sciences--but there are certain definable characteristics: a quest for higher states of consciousness, increased spiritual power and knowledge and direct experience of the divine, as well as the use of procedures, techniques, and practices which draw on hidden or concealed forces to manipulate the empirical course of existence. Nigerians use the term "spiritual sciences" to describe what they consider to be these higher, more mystical and scientific forms of religion. In the West such movements would be described as cults, but that term is inappropriate in the African context since it already refers to traditional religious systems.

The indigenous spiritual science movements must be seen in the light of activities of the imported spiritual science organizations, such as the Rosicrucians (AMORC), Eckankar, the Aetherius Society, Hare Krishna, the Grail Movement, the Subud Brotherhood, the Superet Light Mission, and the Institute of Religious Science.[2] Some of the latter have been active in Nigeria from the 1920s, but the majority have arrived since the end of the Civil War in 1970, brought back by Nigerians resident or traveling overseas, directly through missionary activity or indirectly through the circulation of literature.

The founders of the indigenous spiritual science movements have usually been members of one or more of the above-mentioned organizations, particularly Rosicrucianism. They are not numerous, but we shall refer briefly to three examples that we encountered in Calabar in 1983.

The Spiritual Fellowship was founded in Calabar in 1980 by Mr. A. Peter Akpan, a civil servant and former Methodist, in response to a book he wrote entitled *The Path of Holiness*. The main theme of the book is spiritual development, which the author understands as a graduated path of knowledge by which the student attains higher levels of consciousness, spirituality, and greater power. The author's teachings stem from a variety of religious, mystical, and occult sources; a small group of people gathers weekly to meditate and discuss these teachings.

The founder of the Esom Fraternity Company (Nigeria), Professor Assassu Inyuang-lbom, is a well-known local occultist and mystical specialist who has established a training institution for the "healing arts and sciences" and a "cosmic hospital" just outside of Calabar--the latter is a joint venture of the Society of Metaphysicians in Britain, an American evangelical church, and some Indian associates. A spiritual science movement in the making in Calabar is The Universal Body (TUB). Its founder, an ex-policeman and bar-owner, has received training from the Psychology School of Thought and the Rosicrucians. He is particularly interested in mystical calculations and astrological predictions and receives a stream of callers at his home in the manner of an African guru or modern diviner. He has acquired a plot of land and is amassing the necessary funds to begin construction of a building where people may come and "know what they are worshipping." A former Catholic, Cyril Uwan, maintains that the secrets of Christianity were withheld from the African congregation by the mainly European clergy.[3]

While spiritual science teachings like evangelicalism and pentecostalism have been circulating in Nigeria for many years, notably in the form of books and pamphlets, indigenous movements created solely to systematize and implement these ideas--and not as part of some haphazard or wider syncretism as in the case of several healing homes and spiritual churches--are only just starting to appear. We see them as an increasingly popular phenomenon because of their modern, scientific, neutral (nondenominational), and international aspects as well as their low-key proselytization. We should not overlook their important continuity either with the pragmatism and instrumentalism of the traditional worldview or with concepts such as initiation and esotericism. Their predominant appeal is to the disillusioned male churchgoer who is sufficiently literate and wealthy to have access to the costly resources of the spiritual sciences and who wants a more intellectually stimulating type of religion than the simple ritualism and devotionalism of many of the churches. Another notable aspect of this type of movement is its emphasis on individualism and spiritual self-sufficiency (cf. the Rosicrucian motto: "Your Home is Your Temple"). This is attractive to those who do not want the total or partial commitment demanded by a religious community.

Observations and reflections

In light of the changes described above in the contemporary religious scene in Nigeria, I would like to propose a reformulated typology of new religious movements:
1. Neo-primal movement
2. Healing home
3. Independent church
   a. African church
   b. Spiritual or prophet-healing church
4. Revivalist movement
5. Spiritual science movement

Any typology is evidently an artificial construct and potentially subject to change. The categories have emerged from observable groupings and divisions within the data, with particular reference to the orientation and self-designation of movements themselves.

1. The neo-primal movement is concerned with the revitalization of traditional or primal beliefs and practices. This is usually

characterized by a universalization of the concept of deity and an attempt to transcend regional or ethnic groupings in terms of membership. There is a tendency to reject alien religious forms such as Christianity and Islam.

2. The healing home, or the "prayer house" as it is sometimes called, fits least comfortably into the overall category of new religious movements since it is very much an outgrowth of the traditional healer's compound; the religious content in terms of worship and ritual practices and structures is minimal, since the raison d'être is primarily healing and problem-solving. In terms of structure the healing home seems far from being a movement since it does not seek to expand either through proselytization or publicity. However, there are two reasons why the ubiquitous Nigerian healing home should form part of our typology of new religious movements. First, despite its generally traditional core, the healing home--particularly the urban variety--has a great tendency to eclecticism and syncretism, and it is not uncommon to encounter healing home owners and specialists drawing on a variety of sources such as Christianity, Islam, occultism, Indian magic, astrology, metaphysics, and mysticism. For example, the following notice board was observed in Calabar: "Homeopathic and Botanic Medical Clinic: Occultist, Astrologer and Physician." Second, the recourse to the supernatural is an integral part of the healing home even if it is not expressed in regular worship. Many a healing home and prayer house has developed into a spiritual church.

3a. The African Church is basically an African version of the mission or mainline church, which is why this type of movement is often referred to as orthodox independent or separatist. These churches have retained the polity and liturgy of their parent churches but have advocated African leadership and some African customs such as polygamy.

3b. The spiritual church, or prophet- or prayer-healing church as it is sometimes called because of its emphasis on prophetism and faith-healing, is the most well known of all the new religious movements in Nigeria. From its origins in western Nigeria (where it is known as an Aladura church) it has spread all over the country, propagating a model of religious independency which advocates a rapprochement with African needs, customs, and worldviews. At the same time it draws on Christian teachings and practices to varying degrees and claims a Christian identity.[4]

Our additions to Turner's typology--the revivalist movement and the spiritual science movement--differ from the above types since they rely chiefly on exogenous religious sources for their motivation and inspiration. The concern for indigenization is therefore not paramount even though the adoption process is naturally accompanied by adaptation, and the selection of religious ideas and forms is influenced--if not determined--by affinity with local religious needs and worldviews. The revivalist movement is characterized by such symbols as gospel buses and evangelical tracts rather than by white soutanes and candles. The spiritual science movement, in place of traditional charms, uses Egyptian scarab beetles, Indian talismans, and Tarot cards.

Both types of movements have introduced a new orientation for the new religious movement in Nigeria with their focus on the individual, more informal, looser organizational structures. These features account for their appeal and expansion, for these movements are well suited to serve as potential additives to other types of religious affiliation. The focus on the individual and his or her spiritual development is nurtured not so much through regular ritual participation as through the right reading matter, cassette tapes, or television programs. We may note here also an absence of exclusivism: the individual is encouraged to exploit a variety of sources, whether the writings of other mystics or evangelists, or the American Bible college, or Indian mystical training institution. It is possible also that the fluidity of these movements and their weakly defined boundaries may be encouraging the homogenization of Nigerian religion rather than the pluralization and multiplication of distinct religious collectivities. This observation needs to be discussed at greater length elsewhere.

Like all new religious movements, the revivalist movement and the spiritual science movement reflect the social and religious changes occurring in contemporary Nigeria. With their internationalist and progressive aspirations they are a reflection of the widening religious, social, and cultural horizons of many Nigerians. They constitute an important testimony to the fact that the process of religious self-determination may take several directions and not just the path of Africanization. I therefore consider that the movements described above oblige us to reconsider the definition of the African new religious movement as something thoroughly independent and indigenous both in content and orientation. In addition, the identification of second- and third-generation new religious movements as a response to an "invasive faith" (usually Christianity) seems increasingly inappropriate given the indigenization of Christianity, for example, and the fact that many potential religious innovators are actively seeking new religious forms and ideas overseas. In order to take account of the developments within and variations on our theme, I wish to describe the African new religious movement as "an indigenously created religious organization stemming from social and religious encounter, and selecting and combining local and exogenous elements in diverse and dynamic ways."[5]

There is always much talk in academic circles about the influence of the observer on the observed. In the course of my first visit in 1980 to the headquarters of Calabar's largest spiritual church--the Brotherhood of the Cross and Star--the Sole Spiritual Leader and Founder, Olumba Olumba Obu, having learned that I was from the University of Aberdeen, introduced me to the congregation of over 3,000 people as "Dr. Turner's spiritual daughter!" He then proceeded to praise Harold Turner for his research on the spiritual churches and how he had encouraged students (including Brotherhood members) to continue this important work. By the time Obu had finished his eulogy, "the great Dr. Turner" was a household name and I for one had benefited from my personal connections. I recount this incident--and there are many others--because it not only points to the lasting impression that Harold Turner had made on this particular church leader some 20 years back, but also to the favorable consequences for those who followed in his footsteps and for the dissemination of information on African new religious movements in general. The Brotherhood of the Cross and Star has since welcomed, even encouraged, research into its activities. Like an increasing number of movements, it is developing not just an awareness of its own public and international image but also of likeminded organizations and their importance to scholars of religion and social change and development.

I would like to go one step further and suggest that Harold Turner, through his work and devotion to the field of new religious movements, has himself become--albeit unwittingly!--the founder and guru of a movement of NRM professionals and aficionados. It is a movement which has international connections and a progressive orientation; devotees are required to conduct dedicated field work, to serve as agents of data collection, and to propagate the movement's ideals worldwide. There are no restrictions on membership: all disciplines and confessions are welcomed, and supplementary affiliations are permitted. The rewards are many: a sense of community among members, feedback from the leader, hospitality at the headquarters, and the privilege of being able to contribute to the movement's primary sources such as in this present Festschrift.

NOTES

1. A. A. Dubb gives an account of the African Assembly of East London run by Nicolas Bhengu. The church, which is similar to those described in this section, has a loose association with the Assemblies of God. I am grateful to Professor Bengt Sundkler for drawing my attention to this church.

2. Eleven of these movements (more than ten percent of all distinct religious bodies) were identified during a survey of religious institutions in the town of Calabar (Hackett 1985).

3. This is an important and recurring theme in African religious independency and is treated by Harold Turner (1979c:271-88).

4. I am including in this category the movements which Turner refers to as "Hebraist" or "deviationist" (such as God's Kingdom Society) since these movements, which are few in number, generally prefer to be known as "independent churches." I have also eliminated the category of "syncretist movements" designated by Turner, since this is the least distinctive of all the categories and as he himself says, all movements are to some extent syncretist (Turner 1979a:56).

5. See R. I. J. Hackett (forthcoming) for further discussion of the definitional problem. For definitions by Turner, see Turner (1979d:23; 1984:232).

Rosalind I. J. Hackett

REFERENCES

Concord Weekly
   1985   *Concord Weekly* (Lagos), February 18.
Dubb, A. A.
   1976   *Community of the Saved: An African Revivalist Church in the East Cape*. Johannesburg: Witwatersrand University Press for the African Studies Institute.
Hackett, Rosalind I. J.
   1985   "From Ndem Cults to Rosicrucians: A Study of Religious Change, Pluralism and Interaction in the Town of Calabar, South-Eastern Nigeria," Ph.D. dissertation, University of Aberdeen.
Hackett, Rosalind I. J., ed.
   1987   *New Religious Movements in Nigeria: A Current Perspective*. New York: Edwin Mellin Press.
The Miracles
   1983   "Missionary Journey to India," *The Miracles* (local publication of the TLMI), Vol. 1, (July).
Turner, Harold W.
   1979a   "The Approach to Africa's Religious Movements," *Religious Innovation in Africa: Collected Essays on New Religious Movements*. Boston: G. K. Hall.
   1979b   "A Typology for African Religious Movements," *Religious Innovation in Africa: Collected Essays on New Religious Movements*. Boston: G. K. Hall.
   1979c   "The Hidden Power of the Whites: The Secret Power Withheld from the Primal Peoples," *Religious Innovation in Africa: Collected Essays on New Religious Movements*. Boston: G. K. Hall.
   1979d   "A New Field in the History of Religions," *Religious Innovation in Africa: Collected Essays on New Religious Movements*. Boston: G. K. Hall.
   1984   "New Religious Movements in Primal Societies," *The Penguin Dictionary of Religions*, ed. by John R. Hinnells. Harmondsworth: Penguin.

David A. Shank
Abidjan, Ivory Coast

African Christian religious itinerary:
toward an understanding of the religious itinerary from the faith of African traditional religion(s) to that of the New Testament

The *Alliance Witness* (1983:20) reported as very recent an event not dissimilar to what has been happening in many parts of Africa in the past 150 years. Village Christians in Burkina Faso offered prayer for an aged man and his wife who were harassed by evil spirits. As a result she slept well for the first time in many months, and the next day the man was praising God for answer to prayer. Since the couple wanted to "give themselves to the Lord," the missionary reported, Christians prayed with them and advised him to get rid of all his fetishes. The man, a 70-year-old head of the blacksmith clan and a "leading sorcerer," was baptized the same day, while the Christians and the missionary took "all the idols and fetishes"--more than 25 Christians could carry in one trip--and burned them in a fire that lasted four hours. The other villagers were sullen, terrorized, or tried to obtain a few of the fetishes for themselves before their destruction.

Such an act of faith, with the radical, symbolic break from a religious past, marks the beginning of a new religious itinerary for this aged couple. But what is the nature of that religious itinerary? What is its direction and the content of the evolving religious experience within the new community of African Christians who prayed, baptized, and burned the symbolic past under the tutelage of the Western missionary? Since such events have been occurring countlessly for a century and a half, those experiences and their sequels--personal and collective--constitute the soul of African Christianity,

143

conditioned and solicited by the message of the Bible filtered through the missionary or church communities. There is an inevitable passage from a community canon of oral tradition and experience of spiritual powers to a new religious community with a new approach to power, conditioned by the written canon of Scripture fulfilled in the New Testament. Without questioning the "saving faith" involved in the initial radical break, it would appear important--if only for pastoral reasons[1]--to raise questions about the character of such a religious itinerary with its "stages on life's way."[2]

Such stages are suggested by Dr. H. W. Turner's comprehensive study of the phenomenon of new religious movements in primal societies, first of all in Africa, and then worldwide. His typological description of the whole gamut of movements growing out of the interaction between primal religions and Western Christianity in second-stage responses includes: neo-primal movements, synthetist movements, Hebraist movements, independent churches, and autonomous indigenous churches directly related to missionary endeavor (Turner 1981:49; 1983). In the first-stage response of Africans to Western Christian impact, this range of expression did not appear as such because the religious reality embodied in these types was totally under missionary tutelage within the Christian villages, missionary compounds, or bush churches. Yet, different phases of religious understanding persisted within the new Christian communities, particularly as new Christians joined the churches. That such phases would later appear as independent movements because of the arrangement between colony and mission is, of course, not surprising. What is surprising indeed is that the mission-planted churches would fail to recognize the authenticity of those stages when not under their own tutelage. In any case, the itinerary of the African Christian is clarified by the phenomenological description.

My own reflections on this religious itinerary have grown out of relations with certain parts of the Harrist Church in Ivory Coast, while maintaining simultaneously fraternal relationships and ministry within the larger Christian community. The Harrist Church is not accepted as an authentic Christian church by the rest of the Christian community--whether Roman Catholic, conciliar Protestant, or evangelical--even though it is given serious consideration by national authorities as one of the recognized religious realities, along with Christianity, Islam, and the traditional religions referred to officially as Animism. Yet in my experiences I have discovered among Christians from the "authentic churches" religious understandings similar to those found among the Harrist people I know. These Christians are considered to be authentic because of their belonging to a "proper" church, while the Harrists with Christian understandings are not perceived to be authentic Christians, except perhaps at local, village levels. Late-arrival Western missionary that I was, I found it necessary to ponder on these experiences and observations.[3] The itinerary suggested by Dr. Turner's work was a good starting place for thought, and this article pulls together some of that reflection.

In 1967 a Togolese theologian, Rev. Seth Nomenyo, wrote a little brochure to stimulate thought about the gospel, the church, and the Christian life in view of a churchwide effort of renewal. In it he projected a typical dialogue between "Evangelist" and a "Brother" of the church. If one reads with Dr. Turner's description in mind, one discerns within the Evangelical Church planted by the Bremen Mission the personalizing of a religious itinerary not wholly unlike that model.

Evangelist: My brother, all of the Evangelical Church of Togo is today searching, like you, for the true meaning of the Christian life. It cannot be content simply to follow a certain routine of worship, meetings, holiday festivals, sacraments, collections, and funerals. It wishes to understand what the church is, what the Christian is in our world of today. The answer is in the word which God has given us and which enlightens by his Spirit. Shall we search together? But first of all tell me what you believe you already know about the Christian life.

Brother: For myself, if I am a Christian it is because I have chosen to serve the true God, the God of Jesus Christ, and have rejected the false gods which my fathers worshipped. I believe and I worship the Great God; the pagans worship and serve Satan and his false gods. I belong to God, while the pagans belong to Satan, hence their name: Abossantowo (people of Satan). All the worshippers and servants of the Great God are kept, protected, and helped by him. It is to him that they cry in their distress. On the other hand, the pagans--

servants and worshippers of Satan--trust in him and in his gods and their false priests.

I know that several of my Christian friends have divided hearts; several still believe in the protection of Satan and appeal to him in certain circumstances of their lives, while continuing to call on the true God! I think it is those which are called "[half] Christian, half-pagan."

But why do all men have need to believe in an all-powerful Being whom they can invoke and who delivers them? Because in our world the power of life and the power of death contend for men; these, in their fears, can only desperately seek a refuge in a Being more powerful than death.

Evangelist: You do not speak of Jesus Christ; what place does he fill in your life?

Brother: I'm coming to that. The Christian, after having believed in a Protector-God, discovers a Judge-God--a God in the presence of whom man is sinful and merits punishment. This punishment is hell. To be Christian, therefore, is to flee the punishment of God and to prepare for one's self a place in paradise after death. If I cling so obstinately to the Christian religion, I confess that it is, above all, to make sure of paradise after death. And for that Jesus Christ is very useful. Is he not the Saviour, the one who can wash away my sins, make me evade the punishment of God, and thereby even open for me the gates of paradise?

Evangelist: Thus you believe in the immortality of the human soul?

Brother: Surely! Everyone believes in that: the pagans, the Muslims, the Hindus, the Christians. All men are preparing for that great move which will transport their souls into the abode of the blessed (paradise), or on the contrary, into eternal fire (hell) according to the good pleasure of the gods (or of the Great God).

Evangelist: Are you preparing right now to enter into paradise? What are you doing in order to win heaven, and in order to get in the good graces of God?

Brother: I try to respect the law of God, and to live according to the Christian morals which the church has taught me since my childhood. Thus I've often told myself that the Bible was a book of morals where one finds much counsel about the manner of living, with lists of virtues to practice and of vices to avoid. Then, too, I pay my dues.

Evangelist: Jesus Christ said one day to his disciples: "Blessed are they that are persecuted. . . . As I have been hated, you as well will also be hated." Are the Christians of your village also hated--persecuted by others?

Brother: No, on the contrary. With present-day evolution, Christianity is in style. A civilized man must be a Christian, and many confuse Western civilization with Christianity. If one wants to appear civilized, one must have a Christian name, have his children baptized, participate in memorial services for deceased members of his family, and act on each of these occasions in such a manner as to underline the importance of the family by a show of luxury. Therefore, Christianity in certain cases can be the occasion for a family to be shown off to advantage, to witness to its superiority over other families that are either non-Christians or "mixed."

Evangelist: You are an Eve Christian. I am an Akposso Christian; another is a Christian of Agou, or of Lama-Kara. Does your same faith unite you?

Brother: I must admit that it does not, outside of several exceptions. As for myself, I am Eve first, and then Christian. Perhaps our tribalism is even reinforced by Christianity. There is the church of Agu, the church of Daye, the church of Litime, that of Oblo . . . each living separated from the others by tribal ties which are reinforced by Christian solidarity. For me, to be Christian is also, therefore, to seek to consolidate my tribe by consolidating my church.

Evangelist: My brother, I have heard you. I know that you have been frank, and that is indeed what you believe and what most of the Christians of our church believe. But the truth is not there. We have mixed the Gospel with other beliefs, and in the mixture the salt has lost its savour. We have constructed a religion--a veritable scaffolding--in order for our immortal souls to arrive in paradise . . . [However] the Christian is a person recreated by God in Christ (Nomenyo 1967:12-15; my translation, used by permission of the publisher).

Following Nomenyo, then, one finds a series of phases between the practitioners of traditional religion and the New Testament word: 1) the Christian of a divided heart; 2) the Christian worshiper of the Great All-powerful Protector-God; 3) the Christian discovery of a God of judgment, and the sinful self as punishable; 4) the Christian who uses Christ to guarantee immortality, who practices morality and church rules in order to keep in the good graces of God, and evolves in Westernization, material status, and tribal reinforcement. The New Testament word itself calls for "the person recreated by God in Christ." And according to the theologian, most in the church were in phase four; an all-church program of renewal was being prepared to bring the New Testament word to bear upon the majority within that stage.

A second illustration is provided by Jean-Paul Eschlimann, Roman Catholic missionary in Ivory Coast among the Agni, and a well-informed ethnologist of the Akan ethnic group. He writes of the 11,964 Christians and catechumens in his Mission of Tankessé with its population of 36,000 inhabitants (Eschlimann 1984). Among them, he laments, are only some 50 "Christians" who have faith, i.e., "who have the same trust in Jesus that their brothers give to the customs of the ancestors or to the Koran." The others, though "sacramentalized," continue to put their faith in the ancestral practices. The observer asks, What then is the religious reality of those other 11,900 "Christians"? Is it not essentially a synthesis of Roman sacrament and traditional religion? Indeed, Eschlimann himself complains honestly that as the administrator of the sacraments, he ends up--even though he is a Christian evangelist at heart--by presenting God as immutable, repetitious, legalistic, and particularly concerned about ritual and sacraments--in sum, "a God without a future."

With the use of Turner's model, one might say that a form of Hebraism (a religious reality similar to that of Israel before Christ) is being injected into a synthetist reality, out of which have emerged less than a hundred whose faith in Christ is inscribed in their daily life conduct. Here again are several religious stages between the Western Catholic filter of the Bible with its impact and that of traditional religion. One may, of course, ask whether there was, in the beginning, the same kind of break in power confrontation as that described at the beginning of this text. But, even if it had taken place, experience often proves that after such a break, the pull of the old powers creates a time of intensive tension, testing, and threat of apostasy, as witnessed by a Roman Catholic catechist:

> Say that the fetishes don't have power? No! They do have, and whoever keeps them and wants to reject them immediately because the Father said so, I can assure you that he will not be able to do without them; he is going to return to them.
>
> I had (about two years after his baptism) nevertheless some real times of fear: I'd think, I've thrown my fetishes away, I don't go to the charlatan any more, what is going to happen to me? I said, "Good! I know God is strong, Jesus is powerful." And if I would feel fearful, immediately I would pray. As for that--I say it many times when talking with people--prayer is truly the arm of the Christian. Without prayer, I wonder if I could have resisted and remained Christian like I have.
>
> When I had surmounted that step--for me it was the most diffi-cult--to my surprise there was still another struggle, a struggle with my character. When I hear the Word of God, I leave most saddened because I want to change and I can't succeed. Things like meanness; I was born hard (Deniel 1981:14ff.)[4]

Indeed many do not surmount that step, but it is significant that the Senufo catechist perceived it clearly as a new stage in his faith.

Another illustration of such an itinerary under missionary tutelage is given by John V. Taylor in his study of the church in Buganda. He reports the moving experience of evangelical mission-aries discovering that their

> Christians were not hearing and preaching their clear evangelical emphases as much as they were the news about the transcendant God. "Katonda," the unknown and scarcely heeded creator was pro-claimed as the focus of all life, who yet lay beyond and above the closed unity of all existence. This in itself was so catastrophic a con-cept that, for the majority of hearers, it appeared to be the sum of the new teaching . . . Later on as the same [evangelical] preaching was reiterated, a certain number in the church heard more of it. It is this which accounts for the successive revivals (Taylor 1958:252f).

R. H. Leakey, quoted by Taylor, wrote of the "mission" of 1893: "Many who had long been looked upon as leading Christians real-ized a new force and power in their Christian life. Some said to us, 'Why have you been here so long and never told us this glad news

David A. Shank

before?' All we could say was, 'You have been told but have not believed it.' "

Taylor's comments on this are worth rereading, for they speak to the question of progressive revelation as well as to the problem of religious communication from one cultural platform into another cultural auditorium. Indeed, it is at this point that we part company with Turner's phenomenological description of stages provoked by the impact of Western Christianity. What if the New Testament fulfillment of the Old Testament, rather than Western Christianity, were seen as the impacting pole? This would exclude the too facile identification of Western Christianity--in whatever national, cultural, or denominational wrappings--with the description of New Testament life, experience, and thought whose accents and emphases are often filtered out by Western Christianity's selectivity. How does this New Testament religious faith compare with traditional African religion? If it functions effectively as a conditioning and critiquing canon, what are the stages which it stimulates, solicits, and provokes?

Before attempting an answer to that question, let us look at a situation which was not under missionary tutelage. The event with which we began--an initial break in a context of power confrontation--was given massive expression in 1913-14 when the Glebo prophet from Liberia, W. W. Harris, provoked the baptisms of some 100,000 people after they destroyed the external signs of their traditional religions and turned to the one true and living God as their only recourse. When "discovered" ten years later by British Methodist missionaries, the latter were deeply impressed that all fetish practice had disappeared. Nevertheless, even though they observed that the masses had "replaced heathen superstitions with Christian prayer,"[5] the missionaries constantly raised serious questions about the nature of their religious reality, because of the masses' ignorance of Christ and their biblical illiteracy. Nevertheless, it was a major religious shift. Monica Wilson has written that "a shift from magic to prayer is the great leap in shift from outward forms to inner religion" (Wilson 1971:43).

When Western Christians were asking about the authentic Christian nature of the Kimbanguist Church in Central Africa, the Zairian scholar Martial Sinda insisted--as criticism--that there was not just a

150

simple formal analogy between Kimbanguist and Protestant/Catholic models but that

> ...the break with the traditional religious structures is conscious and significant. The essential religious act has become that of prayer. By simplifying to the extreme, we can say that prayer has replaced sacrifice.
>
> What is represented in this passing over? Sacrifice in traditional Black religion is an efficacious technique; its daily or periodic use is the guarantee of the maintenance of a certain order. The role of individual initiative--that of the gods or that of men--is, if not insignificant, at least always controllable. Thus the strict observance of ritual rules brings about the effective realization of a sought-after result . . ..
>
> In such a perspective, religious anxiety does not exist. Prayer on the contrary, if it remains a religious technique, does not possess the efficaciousness of sacrifice--at least not an immediate efficaciousness. The initiative remains with God, upon Him alone depends the final result of the religious act. This is why religious theory opens out to miracle, and it is also why anxiety sets in at the heart of believers. That this passing over from sacrifice to prayer is accompanied in the believer by a progressive awareness of his responsibility for himself--in a word, of his solitude--illustrates, if it were necessary, the deep gap between Christian religion and the so-called primitive religions (Sinda 1972:90f).

This major shift dominates the first major stage in the itinerary: it is essential to hear how important it is to an African.

A second major shift, with all of its ramifications, is related to what Charles-Daniel Maire calls a change from anthropocentrism to theocentric ethics. The difference between traditional and biblical spiritualities is such that in the latter, the theocentricity of its vision of the world modifies completely the meaning of fault as being that which is against God (1975:138f.). The historian Gordon Haliburton, searching for oral tradition about the Prophet Harris 50 years after his impact, was told by five old men in the village of Petit Bassam, where the mother church of the Harrist Church is located: "When Harris came, the Bible taught us good and evil--sins. [After that] we knew that to kill somebody was a sin. Previously, we knew that it wasn't right, but not the sin aspect" (Haliburton: n.d.). This also means a major shift in an understanding and internalization of personal responsibility. This is so much so that one French anthropologist has severely judged the contemporary Harrist healer Atcho, whose discourse and technique is seen to effect such a displacement. For Marc Augé, the problem of evil--no longer due to the externally attacking spiritual powers--is still external to the individual in new economic and political structures, and not within the individual in society as in certain Christian understandings of original sin (Augé 1975:237-307). It would be overstating the facts to suggest that the forces of modernization and urbanization were just, or played no role whatsoever in the process of individualization taking place in Ivory Coast. But what these do not do, in their secularizing impact, is to produce personal--and internal--responsibility to and before the Creator.

In the context of this stage the Western Christian observer is traditionally overwhelmed by the legalism--both ethical and ritual--despite all efforts to reduce it. However, it would appear rather that Torah was creating a new path out of traditional taboos and prohibitions through the maze of rapid social, economic, cultural, and religious change. In that stage en route, the sacred "house of God," where one can act "before God,"[6] as well as the mediating priest, pastor, or missionary are often also seen as an integral part of that educational process. And that new way, despite the Westerners' contrary understanding, is perceived by the participants as a gift from God.

A further major stage is where the grace and the Spirit of God are known as presence of Christ-in-community, a free obedient expression of the coming kingdom of God, demonstrated in the personalized gifts and potential in the service of the peace, justice, healing, and reconciliation of the new creation. This stage of eschatological faith drove the prophet Harris beyond the bounds of the Western missionary model and enabled the breakthrough into a new itinerary for thousands. He did not communicate that religious phase to those people in the countless villages; but he had himself undergone an itinerary of more than 30 years before entering it. Many of his disciples today might indeed be seen as Hebraist.

One may be struck with certain parallels between such an itinerary and that of Israel, led in covenant to the "fullness of times."

One recalls how the Apostle Paul saw the faith of Abraham, David, and Habakkuk--and his own faith--as part of a common itinerary of saving faith (Rom 1-4), yet all were expressed within different contexts of religious perception and understandings in which God had revealed himself and solicited faith. The illustration from Uganda suggests that the gospel, the preaching of Christ, the word of grace, and the good news of the kingdom tend to be perceived differently at each stage as new response is made to that word.

It is thus not surprising that African evangelical theologians write openly of how the gospel of Christ is capable of "meeting the primal man at the points of his greatest need" in a "process or processes of 'power encounter' between the Christian and the primal worldviews" (Thailand Report 1980:15-18). In an approach which they have outlined, there is a "gradual unfolding of Christian truth," where Christian understandings of sin, deliverance, humans gone astray, belief and trust in God as revealed in Christ "begin to open up," "begin to be appreciated," "begin to be apprehended"; the primal person "begins to see," "begins to realize." This is the language of itinerary which is not native to the typical Western evangelical.[7]

Were we to set up a cursory description of African traditional religions on the one hand, and a parallel description of New Testament religion on the other, we might suggest a typical itinerary somewhat according to the following pattern:

David A. Shank

A religious itinerary from African traditional religion to New Testament faith

1. AFRICAN TRADITIONAL RELIGIONS

a. Reign of the ancestors (traditions, the elders, orality)
b. Creator God, distant and unknown (believed in without experience)
c. Tribe, clan, family (birth and initiation)
d. "Life" means power, prosperity, fertility, success (maintained through harmony and equilibrium via repression, submission, compensation)
e. Totem, taboo (fear, submission)
f. Good spirits: divinities, genies, "living dead" (sacrifices and ritual for blessing and prosperity)
g. Evil-doing spirits: divinities, genies, "living dead" (sacrifices and ritual for protection)
h. Diviners, "fetishers," religious specialists (divination, possession, mediation, revelation in dreams, visions, trances)
i. Witchcraft and magic (expose and destroy the guilty; protection through sacrifice, ritual, fetish)
j. Festival, ritual (necessary, efficacious celebration)
k. Reincarnation (discerned after birth)
l. After-life: village of the dead, spiritual counterpart to here and now
m. Present life: duty, roles, past traditions, cyclical
n. Myth dominant: preexistent story of life and existence
o. Shame a dominant undercurrent, in response to socio-cultural pressures

2. PROCESS OF GRADUAL APPROPRIATION OF CHRISTIAN TRUTH: NEW APPREHENSIONS, NEW APPRECIATIONS

Conversion to all-powerful God (compared to less-powerful entities) * *	Struggle to abandon old sources of power and protection * *	Law of God and Bible and cult replace fetishes and taboo * *	Discovery of personal responsibility before God and fellow humans	Discovery of grace of God revealed in Christ	Discovery of life in the Spirit — Gifts and fruits of the Spirit	Discovery of the Church as community of the Spirit and sign in the world of the coming Kingdom
Present and active * *						
One true God is tested over and over again * *	Constant threat to apostasize * *	God requires WORSHIP in sacred place * *	Disquiet and anguish because of sinfulness within, incapacity to avoid sin or to do good * *	* *	Gifts and fruits of the Spirit * *	
Known through his acts of power and protection for "health, prosperity, fertility, success in this-life" * *		Religious specialist is necessary for mediation of God's power concerning law of church, discipline, forgiveness * *			Freedom * *	

DEEP CONCERN FOR AFTER-LIFE .... DEEP CONCERN FOR NEW CREATION/MISSION IN WORLD
DEEP APPRECIATION FOR OLD COVENANT .... DEEPENING APPRECIATION OF THE NEW COVENANT
POWER SIGNS ARE VERY SIGNIFICANT .... MINISTRY OF THE WORD AND TEACHING VERY SIGNIFICANT
PRAYER REPLACES SACRIFICES .... LIBERATION FROM LEGALISM AND FORMALISM
(a major shift ... with mastery)
SHAME DOMINANT .... GUILT INCREASINGLY IMPORTANT
SPIRIT AS PUNCTUAL INTERVENTION .... SPIRIT AS CHRIST-PRESENCE

3. NEW TESTAMENT FAITH

a. Kingdom of God, present and coming (Bible, Church, Holy Spirit)
b. Redeemer God, revealed in Christ (faith/commitment to purpose; communal worship)
c. The Church, the people of God (new birth, baptism, Lord's Supper, based on personal decision)
d. "Life" means service, justice, peace, holiness, freedom (life in Christ, life in the Spirit via repentance, forgiveness, acceptance)
e. Christ and his teaching, the fulfillment of God's Law (love-obedience, discipleship, participation)
f. Angels: fellowship of the saints (thanksgiving, rejoicing)
g. Satan vanquished, with demons and evil spirits (faith, prayer, exorcism, fellowship)
h. The Church, a community of gifts (charisms) (fellowship, sharing, intercession, discernment of dreams, visions, trances)
i. Providence, intervention of God, mutual aid of the congregation (forgiveness for guilty; and trust, hope, prayer, healing)
j. Festival, ritual (voluntary celebration for edification)
k. Resurrection (hope, expectation after death)
l. After-life: fulfillment of God's purposes for peace, justice, unity
m. Present life: anticipatory expression of future hope; linear
n. History dominant: story of God's redeeming acts and promises in fulfillment
o. Guilt a dominant undercurrent, in response to internal pressures

(For detailed reading, see Appendix at the end of this chapter.)

In such a perspective, one would discover in Catholic, Protestant, and evangelical as well as in independent milieus many people in different stages en route--on the way. The manner in which the New Testament canon is screened through preaching, worship, institutions, charisms, traditions, ritual, and doctrine obviously conditions its effectiveness in soliciting and provoking to a further stage on the way. Some movements, as well as individual persons within them, will be blocked in a phase because of the way canonical reality is ignored, excluded, distorted, or disobeyed.

At the same time such a typical itinerary indicates nothing about the length of time which a person or a group may spend within a given stage. Illumination with commitment may happen repeatedly in rapid succession; or it may happen rapidly at one stage and be delayed at others. Neither does the suggested itinerary indicate a natural religious evolution; implicit at each stage is the input from the biblical canon, new understandings, and illumination based on previous experience followed by commitment. Each time a new religious reality is produced a new spirituality is born. Appropriate here is the description of John V. Taylor's "three aspects of the creative activity of the Holy Spirit, the Lord, the Giver of Life."

> From within the depths of its being he urges every creature again and again to take one more tiny step in the direction of higher consciousness and personhood; again and again he creates for every creature the occasion for spontaneity and the necessity for choice, and at every turn he opposes self-interest with a contrary principle of sacrifice, or existence for the other. And, in the fullness of time, this was perfectly disclosed in Jesus Christ who was conceived by the Holy Spirit and to whom the Holy Spirit has been directing men's attention ever since (Taylor 1972:36).

This itinerary does not answer the question of whether it is possible to skip a stage en route. Godfrey Phillips, following the analogy of the progressive revelation of God in Israel's history, insists that no stage can be skipped (Phillips 1942:95ff.). Indeed the African Evangelical theologians in their suggested process imply that the "legalistic" stage could be skipped, since it is the result of missionary failure: starting "with a moral code from a 'God' whom they [Africans] hardly understood or trusted, thus producing 'Christians' who spent the rest of their lives trying to obey God and be good by

David A. Shank

pleasing the missionaries or pastors, only to fail at every turn" (Thailand Report 1980:17). Phillips had turned the equation around by writing of the church "whose teachers give it the Gospel without first giving it the law, and are surprised to find that it interprets the Gospel as if it were law, misses the whole point of divine redemption, and produces an essentially legalistic Christianity" (1942:95f). One is tempted to conclude that any stage which is skipped over will ultimately be experienced at a later time. In that sense, the stages as suggested may not always be the exact order of experience. When I suggested elsewhere (Shank 1983:55-66) that the "legalism" experienced by Westerners in much of African Christianity is such a "stage" in a divine pedagogy of salvation, this was helpfully contested in the name of the Apostle Paul who denounced the "backward" legalistic movement of the Galatians who had been bewitched (Béarth, 1983:78-80). Yet from the perspective of missionary experience and history, one might ask whether the Galatians initially understood and experienced Paul's preaching of Christ's grace, the Spirit, and gospel freedom in the same way that he did, when they first believed. In fact, Paul was doing his missionary task by bringing the New Testament gospel and canon to bear upon a stage that he himself had experienced and transcended.

From the perspective of this suggested itinerary, when in the initial power confrontation Christ is fully trusted, at each succeeding stage he will be experienced differently: the More Powerful, the Faithful Protector, the new Law-giver, the Holy One, the Giver of grace and life, the Ever-present, the Creator of a new humanity. Is this indeed the answer to the questions I raised about the religious itinerary of the 70-year-old fetisher-head of the blacksmith clan in a village of Burkina Faso? If so, at every stage Christ is good news, and at every new stage he brings renewed freedom.

But this is a description by a Westerner. An African Christian, minister of state in his country, put the African religious itinerary somewhat differently:

> The way which leads to God is his own Word. This way is long, very long, and is set like a ladder which is visible from any point, but whose bottom and top rungs are invisible. Nevertheless, when one steps on a rung--at whatever level--and willingly hangs on, the Spirit of God Himself progressively unveils to the climber the different

ruⁿgs behind and before which permit him to advance and to reach him at the Kingdom of Light and Life where He awaits us (Ekra 1977:16).

Here is a vertical ladder--rung after rung--instead of a forward itinerary--stage after stage; both images catch the essential note of new response to new illumination. But the direction is not a secondary question; the Western church itself was sidetracked for many years on a ladder reaching to a God without a future.

NOTES

1. Other reasons: the dynamics and meaning of religious change, the African experience of Christianization--as insight into developments within Western Christianity, et al.

2. We recall Sören Kierkegaard's nineteenth-century religious analysis of Westerners as moving from the aesthetic, to the ethical, to the religious; the contemporary American theologian, John Dunne, writes of the immediate man, the existential man, and the historical man. More recently, but in a different light, Fowler has invited us to look at the "stages of faith" in the Western context.

3. I went to sub-Sahara Africa for the first time in 1971, visiting the Kimbanguists at their 50th anniversary celebration, and have worked with African Independent Churches more directly since 1979, after a 23-year ministry in Belgium from 1950-73, a brief stint as religion professor in the United States, and further study at the University of Aberdeen.

4. Ten small brochures in the series give unusual insight into the religious experience of Catholic Christians at the grassroots.

5. The description by missionary Pierre Benoît, at the time of his 1926 meeting with the Prophet Harris at Cape Palmas, Liberia.

6. Here also Dr. Turner has done pioneering work in phenomenology of religious architecture (1979:chs 2,3).

7. One of the African participants explained how a Western theologian present at the discussion could not conciliate this African perception with his own evangelical doctrine of regeneration and tried to have this particular section deleted from the final draft of the findings.

David A. Shank

REFERENCES

Augé, Marc
  1975   *Théorie des pouvoirs et ideologie*. Paris: Hermann.
Alliance Witness
  1983   *Alliance Witness*, the periodical of The Christian and
          Missionary Alliance, 118:9, April 27.
Béarth, Thomas
  1983   "Pédagogie divine et cheminement humain: un piege
          missiologique?" *Perspectives Missionnaires*, 6.
Deniel, Raymond
  1981   *Chemins de Chrétiens Africains 2*. Abidjan: INADES.
Ekra, Mathieu
  1977   *L'échelle sans fin*. Abidjan: NEA.
Eschlimann, Jean-Paul
  1984   In René Luneau, Lettre No. 10, *Afrique et Parole*,
          November.
Haliburton, Gordon
  n.d.   Personal notes.
  1971   *The Prophet Harris*. London: Longmans.
Maire, Charles-Daniel
  1975   *Dynamique sociale des mutations religieuses*, mémoire of
          1975. Sorbonne: E.P.H.E.
Nomenyo, Seth
  1967   Tout l'Evangile à tout l'Homme. Yaoundé: CLE.
Phillips, Godfrey
  1942   *The Old Testament in the World Church*. London and
          Redhill: Lutterworth.
Shank, David A.
  1983   "Une réponse imprévue à l'action missionnaire,"
          Perspectives Missionnaires, 6.
Sinda, Martial
  1972   *Messianisme Congolais*. Paris: Payot.
Taylor, John V.
  1972   *The Go-Between God*. London: SCM.
Thailand Report
  1980   "Thailand Report," *Christian Witness to People of
          African Traditional Religion*, No. 18. Wheaton: Lausanne
          Committee on World Evangelization.

David A. Shank

Turner, Harold W.
  1979   *From Temple to Meeting House*. The Hague: Mouton.
  1981   "Religious Movements in Primal (or Tribal) Societies,"
          Mission Focus, 9:3.
  1983   "A Further Frontier for Missions: A General Introduc-
          tion to New Religious Movements in Primal Societies,"
          Missionalia, 11:3.
Wilson, Monica
  1971   *Religion and Transformation of Society*. Cambridge:
          University Press.

David A. Shank

1. AFRICAN TRADITIONAL RELIGIONS

a. Reign of the ancestors (traditions, the elders, orality)
b. Creator God, distant and unknown (believed in without experience)
c. Tribe, clan, family (birth and initiation)
d. "Life" means power, prosperity, fertility, success (maintained through harmony and equilibrium via repression, submission, compensation)
e. Totem, taboos (fear, submission)
f. Good spirits: divinities, genies, "living dead" (sacrifices and ritual for blessing and prosperity)
g. Evil-doing spirits: divinities, genies, "living dead" (sacrifices and ritual for protection)
h. Diviners, "fetishers," religious specialists (divination, possession, mediation, revelation in dreams, visions, trances)
i. Witchcraft and magic (expose and destroy the guilty; protection through sacrifice, ritual, fetish)
j. Festival, ritual (necessary, efficacious celebration)
k. Reincarnation (discerned after birth)
l. After-life: village of the dead, spiritual counterpart to here and now
m. Present life: duty, roles, past traditions, cyclical
n. Myth dominant: preexistent story of life and existence
o. Shame a dominant undercurrent, in response to socio-cultural pressures

2. PROCESS OF GRADUAL APPROPRIATION OF CHRISTIAN TRUTH: NEW APPREHENSIONS, NEW APPRECIATIONS

Conversion to all-powerful God (compared to less-powerful entities)	Struggle to abandon old sources of power and protection	Law of God and Bible and cross replace fetishes and taboos	Discovery of personal responsibility before God and fellow humans	Discovery of grace of God revealed in Christ	Discovery of life in the Spirit	Discovery of the Church as community of the Spirit and sign in the world of the coming Kingdom
**	**	**	**	**	**	
Present and active **	Constant threat to apostasize ***	God *requires* WORSHIP in sacred place **	Disquiet and anguish because of sinfulness within, incapacity to avoid sin or to do good **		Gifts and fruits of the Spirit ***	
Known through his acts of power and protection for health, prosperity, fertility, success in this-life **	One true God is tested over and over and over again ***	Religious specialist is necessary for mediation of God's power concerning law of church, discipline, forgiveness ***			Freedom **	

DEEP CONCERN FOR AFTER-LIFE .... DEEP CONCERN FOR NEW CREATION/MISSION IN WORLD
DEEP APPRECIATION FOR OLD COVENANT .... DEEPENING APPRECIATION OF THE NEW COVENANT
POWER SIGNS ARE VERY SIGNIFICANT .... MINISTRY OF THE WORD AND TEACHING VERY SIGNIFICANT
PRAYER REPLACES SACRIFICES .... LIBERATION FROM LEGALISM AND FORMALISM
(a major shift . . . with anxiety)
SHAME DOMINANT .... GUILT INCREASINGLY IMPORTANT
SPIRIT AS PUNCTUAL INTERVENTION .... SPIRIT AS CHRIST-PRESENCE

David A. Shank

3. NEW TESTAMENT FAITH

a. Kingdom of God, present and coming (Bible, Church, Holy Spirit)

b. Redeemer God, revealed in Christ (faith/commitment to purpose; communal worship)

c. The Church, the people of God (new birth, baptism, Lord's Supper, based on personal decision)

d. "Life" means service, justice, peace, holiness, freedom (life in Christ, life in the Spirit via repentance, forgiveness, acceptance)

e. Christ and his teaching, the fulfillment of God's Law (love-obedience, discipleship, participation)

f. Angels; fellowship of the saints (thanksgiving, rejoicing)

g. Satan vanquished, with demons and evil spirits (faith, prayer, exorcism, fellowship)

h. The Church, a community of gifts (charisms) (fellowship, sharing, intercession, discernment of dreams, visions, trances)

i. Providence, intervention of God, mutual aid of the congregation (forgiveness for guilty; and trust, hope, prayer, healing)

j. Festival, ritual (voluntary celebration for edification)

k. Resurrection (hope, expectation after death)

l. After-life: fulfillment of God's purposes for peace, justice, unity

m. Present life: anticipatory expression of future hope; linear

n. History dominant: story of God's redeeming acts and promises in fulfillment

o. Guilt a dominant undercurrent, in response to internal pressures

Walter J. Hollenweger

University of Birmingham

The theological challenge of indigenous churches

This article does not discuss the amazing numerical growth, vitality, and diversity of non-white indigenous churches (as David Barrett calls them) or new religious movements (as Harold Turner calls them). It looks rather at the challenge of these churches for our own theological thinking.

In general the growth of the indigenous churches is part and parcel in the shift of the center of gravity of Christianity from the West to the South. **The first challenge** of these indigenous churches is therefore for us **to recognize a return of Christianity to its roots.** The Christian Church started as a third-world church, and it may well be that it is again becoming predominantly a third-world church. Therefore we should not be astonished that some of the leading officers of the world church (at least in the Protestant denominations) come from the third world. Two general secretaries of the World Council of Churches came from younger churches (Philip Potter from the Caribbean, Emilio Castro from Uruguay). The leaders of both the Lutheran World Federation and the World Alliance of Reformed Churches come from younger churches (Josiah M. Kibira from Tanzania, Allan Boesak from South Africa).

We might better understand this process if we remember the transfer of Christianity from the old Palestinian mother church to the young Hellenistic mission church of the first century. We might also be warned by history that a church which stubbornly remains within the confines of its biblical tradition--as was the case with the Jewish Christians--is digging its own grave.

Walter J. Hollenweger

The second challenge is the search for a new ecumenical and intercultural theology. In the past each nation, each culture, and each religion had its own history, its own roots, and its own future. History was lived in the plural as the different histories of more or less independent entities. Today, however, we still might have our different pasts, our traditions of the past, but we have only one future (in the singular). Only those religions which can represent in their liturgy and theology this common world history, this common future, can claim to be world religions.

From this it follows that non-white indigenous churches will have to work together with the rest of the churches for a common future. It is no longer desirable that each church works towards its own indigenous theology and liturgy but much more that their indigenous theology and liturgy is presented as a part of a **common ecumenical** theology and history.

That, however, is so far not the case. One can describe what is happening in the following simplified alternatives. First, the younger churches in the third world are subsidized *ad infinitum* by the Western churches which finance a ministry trained and functioning according to the Western pattern, Western theological education, church organizations, and medical institutions.

Second, inspired by the non-white indigenous churches, the younger churches forego their support in finance and people from the West and develop their own theology and church structure, including an educational system and a health service which is informed by their own indigenous tradition. The most impressive examples of this development are some non-white indigenous churches and also the churches of China--it is said that their membership has tripled since the missionaries were withdrawn.

Neither approach takes the biblical message seriously enough. In both cases the challenge of the relationship between contextuality and particularity, between the indigenous and the universal dimension of the church, is bypassed. In the one case, this happens through officially denied yet in practice powerful financial and theological dependence. In the other case, it happens through total isolation from the Western churches.

The biblical authors were contextual theologians in the sense that the elements which they adopted into their thinking were integrated after a rigorous selection-and-reinterpretation process. In this we have to follow them. The criteria for what is acceptable and what is not are found not solely in the Bible but equally in dialogue--and if need be in controversy--with the whole catholic church.

The same criteria are valid for Western theology in relation to insights and discoveries of the indigenous churches. The dialogue between these churches is as necessary for Western churches as it is for third-world churches--and this in the interests of a relevant and indigenous Western theology. This is true not only for missiology but equally for pastoral, systematic, moral, and biblical theology. In the latter disciplines, the relevance of the theology of indigenous churches has scarcely been acknowledged. There are still far too many biblical scholars who have no idea of the hermeneutical tools of black churches in the United States and in the United Kingdom. Too many pastoral theologians know nothing of the process of communication in a Zionist church or the liturgical tradition in the Cherubim and Seraphim churches; too many systematic theologians are unaware that there are ways of expressing the coherence of the Christian witness other than those we have developed in the West.

The third challenge is the search for the practicalities of such an intercultural theology. Practical encounter is hindered when even the selection of the theological language is a fundamental theological decision--something which becomes evident in any seminar where non-white indigenous church leaders and Western theologians take part. If we choose the propositional terminology and definitions of the West, any third-world theologian would find it difficult to make specific contributions. On the other hand, if we choose the oral, narrative language of the younger churches, the theologians of the West find it difficult to make a contribution. In practical terms the Western language is almost always used, leading to the suppression of experience and facts which can be expressed only in oral language. Here the insight of W. Wink becomes obvious: "Even the choice of syntax and vocabulary is a political [and I might add 'a theological'] act that defines and circumscribes the way 'facts' are to be experienced--indeed, in a sense even creates the facts that can be studied" (Wink 1973:8; see also Hollenweger 1981:155-79).

A solution is possible only if theologians--and not just missiologists--become bilingual. This should be all the easier since the oral,

Walter J. Hollenweger

narrative language is well known to theologians through biblical scholarship.

Three topics are particularly important for such an ecumenical theology.

Dreams and visions. Most Christians of the third world have become Christians through dreams, visions, apparitions of ancestors, healings, and similar experiences, and seldom indeed on the basis of catechism or a sermon. That does not mean that catechism and sermons are unimportant, but they are not vital for somebody becoming a Christian. How can these third-world Christians take our theology seriously if we do not take seriously that which is the existential foundation of their Christianity? A biblical critique is part and parcel of this serious dialogue. Gabriel Setiloane complains bitterly that even the WCC left out a passage on the important function of ancestors in one of his articles. Furthermore, we Europeans also have to learn again to relate to our ancestors (see the many tombs in Anglican and Roman Catholic churches) our visions, and our dreams. To devalue them theologically and leave them to psychology, psychiatry, or parapsychology means to forego one's theological responsibility on a subject which is as important as moral or doctrinal theology. That such a study would throw up serious questions in our understanding of scholarship and theology is no reason to bypass it. On the contrary it could help us inaugurate an important paradigm-shift (Kuhn). Such a paradigm-shift might show us that secularization is a passing local affair.

Healing of the sick. For non-white indigenous churches some form of healing the sick in church services is paramount. For them sickness is immediately a symptom of a deficient social relationship to people, to nature, to the ancestors, or to oneself. Therefore a medical treatment which sees sickness as a physical deficiency only, which isolates a patient in a hospital bed when he or she most needs the support of friends, co-religionists and family, appears as a grotesque superstition of the ignorant white person who confuses the symptoms with the illness. Most non-white indigenous churches started because of a controversy on this issue. A fundamental dialogue on this issue is all the more important since the World Health Organization in Geneva also recognizes the one-sidedness, and in fact the dangerous incompetence, of the Western health industry and

166

searches for third world alternatives. In any case, we can learn from these churches that healing is part of the liturgy, i.e., it belongs in the public services of the church and not merely to the pastoral care for the individual.

Propositional and oral communication. The Nobel Peace Prize winner, Desmond Tutu from South Africa, says that his theology can only be expressed adequately in song, story, and dance. It is interesting that for Tutu the locus of theology is the liturgy of the church--a very old insight of the Christian church which we seem to forget, to our own disadvantage. Here again Western theologians have to become bilingual if they want to be competent Western theologians and not merely the religious rationalizers of the Western tribes to which they happen to belong.

Harold Turner's life work and documentation centre in the Selly Oak Colleges is of the utmost importance, not just for future missionaries but also for theological thinkers in Europe who want to break out of our European parochialism, because he provides us with a wealth of information on a way of theology which is foreign to us but in many instances akin to the roots of Christianity.

REFERENCES
Hollenweger, Walter J.
    1981   "The Other Exegesis," *Horizons in Biblical Theology* 3.
Wink, W.
    1973   *The Bible in Human Transformation: Toward a New Paradigm for Biblical Study*. Philadelphia: Fortress Press.

Walter J. Hollenweger

Carl F. Starkloff, S. J.

Regis College, University of Toronto

The new primal religious movements: towards enriching theology as hermeneutic

"We are partly responsible for the existence of such movements: they therefore belong to the Christian story" (Turner 1981:54).

In the course of some fifteen years, by means at times painful and at times pleasurable, I have learned that a theology of the oppressed cannot be written by one not of their number, however supportive and sympathetic the writer may be. The oppressed, it is said today, must articulate their own history and do their own theology. In this light, may the theologians from the so-called mainstream, from the establishment, do anything to be of assistance? The answer is that, since we are all part of the Christian story, the theologian from the sending church has both the call and the opportunity to create a working theology of mutual collaboration that will nourish the process of authentic church growth. Further, as the theologian returns again to the sources of Christian tradition--basically and uniquely to Holy Scripture--and to the experiences of tribal people caught up in the historical movement in which Christianity has played a large part, that theologian's call is to develop a systematic that will be a deeper and better informed hermeneutic of the sources--of "the religious classics," as David Tracy calls them (Tracy 1981:130), and of the living context of the people in emerging tribal societies.

In the enquiry after such a hermeneutic, the Christian theologian should return again to biblical sources. My approach here, however,

169

Carl F. Starkloff, S. J.

begins with a philosophical interpretation of history through a
dialectic which, in its broad outlines, may serve as a phenomenology
of the church's experience of the new movements--a diachronic
interpretation of the phenomena. I am, of course, speaking of a
graced dialectic maintained in a continuity by God; grace perseveres
in creation through God's free and faithful self-gift even when sin
has distorted that image and likeness given by the Creator. We thus
work out of a retrieval of Irenaeus' theology of recapitulation in
Christ (St. Irenaeus 5, 6, 1; 6, 9, 1).[1]

The thesis of this dialectic of the church's mission to tribal peoples is the meeting of Christian proclamation with primal peoples in
their own search for the Divine (de Lubac 1967; Rahner 1982:1-137;
Rahner 1965:297-317). Our method is thus grounded in the position
that all religions contain some elements beyond the merely magical
and pragmatic, some aspiration for transcendence, and some related
ethical consciousness. But as a Christian and a realist, the theologian
recognizes sin in all those forms that have somehow lost the primor-
dial thrust towards unity, and this within Christianity as well as in the
other religions. Thus, the dialectic manifests itself through a confession of sin on the part of the church, shown especially as pride in the
form of cultural arrogance. Whatever of sin there may have been
within the primal societies encountered by the gospel (granted the
testimony of Paul in Romans 1-2) will not be matter for this article,
however; once again, those people alone are in the position to name
their own sins. It is for the church, in turn, to name its own sins.

The dialectic of grace and sin manifests itself in the antithesis
shown in the new or independent movements, described recently in
Missiology (1985). It is of great importance that the church recognize
that grace is indeed operative in those movements, as it was in the
primal religions, in which "answers to those profound mysteries of
the human condition" were sought (Abbot 1966:661). It is also
important to remind ourselves that the new movements are generally
some form of Christ-confession and acts of obedience to the Holy
Spirit, however much division may remain. Yes, these movements
manifest themselves phenomenologically as heresy, but the classic
interpretation of heresy is that it always contains a portion of the
truth. It is the theologian's task to discover that portion of the truth,
both in explicit statements and, equally important, in what each new

movement tells the church about itself. It is then the hermeneutical process of theologians from all traditions involved to search for the synthesis--the new truth, the higher truth, purged of sin and heresy. This synthesis thus becomes a "mediated immediacy" of new whole-ness in the experience of both reflection and spontaneity, where tra-dition and enthusiasm come together. The church will have learned from its dissident members and advanced another step towards authentic catholicity.

The message of this essay is directed, first of all, to the missionary theologian. We shall dwell therefore on the conversion--intellectual, moral, religious, and psychic--of the church.[2] In order to appreciate this need to recognize and respect the process of slow and healthy growth--and so to forgive ourselves as well as our partners in dia-logue--our theology must draw from the metaphors of Scripture as well as from the kinds of Christology offered by the New Testament. In a previous article (Starkloff 1985:94-96), I proposed three basic themes that might serve as a basis for dialogue between the "mother churches" and the new movements. These themes are the Living God, Jesus Christ, and the New Creation. These are chosen because 1) they are common themes in nearly all these groups, and 2) because in these themes we possess the substance of Jesus' preach-ing in terms that focus on native religious experience as it has occurred since contact with European missions.

The above-mentioned article also urges that 3) a policy of gradu-alism be a priority in this dialogue, as opposed to the haste of earlier evangelism. Our sense of urgency must be turned from a zeal for a return to the fold of these communities--in light of the presence of grace in their midst--to a secular zeal to work together for the unifi-cation of believers in the divine saving will, and thence to a zeal for the achievement of one human community. Transcendent salvation is no less a priority, but gradualism takes the faith-risk that the final recapitulation will be better served through our collaboration in preparing all cultures to enter it in their integrity as well as in their brokenness.

We must add to this theology 4) the element of pneumatology. Contemporary Christian theologians are examining with greater attention a deepening of the sense of the Holy Spirit at work outside the boundaries of the visible church (Khodr 1981:36-49; Schlette

1966). A fortiori, in such communities where the search for the love of God, the healing presence of Jesus, and the concern for the New Creation are dominant aspirations, one may discern the operation of the Spirit. Recent reflections on the thought of the late Bernard Lonergan emphasize the role of the Holy Spirit as he (perhaps more fittingly in this case expressed as "she") moves gently and gradually in various religions, thus balancing the more aggressive mode of traditional Word-centered evangelization.[3] The parable of the mustard seed comes to mind; the kingdom is seen as still growing slowly within the life of the new movements, even though they may not conform fully to the traditional forms of doctrinal integrity within the sending churches.

The explicit Christology of such a theology would find its formulation in New Testament imagery as well, responding with identificationist rather than extractionist methods (Kraft 1978:151-55) and with a spirit of mutuality in service. A "Christology from below" would better express the experience of the new movements, which have sought a Savior who accepts and shares rather than rejects their culture, and who champions their right to be who they are. This Jesus is portrayed in the teaching and suffering of his public life as a member of a particular culture (Segundo 1973:3-23). Yet an empathetic handling of a "Christology from above" will also proclaim the kenotic Christ of Philippians 2:5-11, who surrenders the power possessed in his being "in the morphé of God," accepting the consequences of involvement in a local culture, including death at the hands of that culture when he challenged it in its most sensitive areas. It is no domesticated "Christ of culture" here, but a transforming Christ who works from within (Niebuhr 1951:ch 3,6), in the persons of local prophets and agents of change. Evangelization in this light is not preaching from a platform of temporal power, which has so often contributed to the demise of a culture in such a way that revitalization is forced to exclude Christ; it proclaims from the position of one who shares the pilgrimage. Christ is found at the heart of all that is good in such movements, which, one might add, constitute preeminent examples of those "semiotic domains" sought by Robert Schreiter in his work on local theologies (Schreiter 1985:61-70).

In pursuit of a holistic theology, we must examine the relationship between ecclesiology and eschatology. If church is to be a genuine experience of religious belonging, it must offer tribal peoples a structural totality that Tillich called a "Gestalt of grace" (Tillich 1948,1966:202-21), a total and communal environment animated by the Divine Presence, a substance that is authentic religion and a form that is a dynamic cultural configuration. Of course, the mission church may have to live with some ambiguity as to the purity of the relationship between form and content in ritual, preaching, and ethics--something it has always had to do in mission situations, in any case. While a careful employment of religious phenomenology, psychology, anthropology, and theology will be important in arriving at authentic native Christianity, missiologists may also have to yield a bit of the syncretophobia that has generally haunted their reflections.

A dialogical theology will also be discerningly contemplative as it strives to articulate the unfolding of the mystery of the Word in creation and in history--the mystery of humankind joining with all creation in growth towards fulfillment. The tragedy of the more revolutionary and apocalyptic religious movements was that their hope was for a return to a lost paradise and that hope was crushed by superior fire power. Christian theology is a hermeneutic that stresses a proleptic eschatology; analogously to the new movements which strove and still strive to prefigure the New Creation in their communal forms, the Church must embody the Gestalt of grace that bears living witness to all that is hopeful and valuable in the tribal cultures and religions.

In the light of what has been said, a contemporary "handmaid" of theology will be the phenomenology of religion, especially as represented by G. Van der Leeuw (1963), Mircea Eliade (1961, 1967), Joachim Wach (1966), and Rudolf Otto (1967). Theology will obtain its language and imagery-symbol through the exercise of careful descriptive and interpretative classification provided by these authors. Theology will learn anew how to articulate the experience of divine disclosure in the events of the new religious movements. Gibson Winter has compared the work of theology to the artistic process (Winter's own "root metaphor")[4] as it creates the imagery of a people's self-interpretation in living symbolism:

1. Theology must interpret symbol as event rather than thing, just as the forms of the new movements have been dynamic realities and

not merely outward forms: this means that form embodies power, in the words of Van der Leeuw.

2. Theology will articulate symbols as both calling forth reflection and stimulating to action, so that the churches will develop processes of theological reflection as pastoral praxis.

3. Theology will use symbols to join together past and future, to illustrate to tribal peoples how Christianity honors and fulfills their ancient traditions even as it promises a hopeful future.

4. Theology must be the critical process that can deal with the multi-faceted nature of symbols, to prevent confusion in the work of inculturation, and to forestall vulgar exploitation of authentic symbolic life, as so often happens to North American Indian culture.

In sum, it is the work of theology to place all symbolism ever more at the service of the Spirit, who alone can effect its mediation of the Word of God.

Finally, David Tracy has proposed a threefold typology of theology that may be especially serviceable to a missiology to tribal religious dialogue. Tracy sees theologies as being either 1) manifestation (disclosure), 2) proclamation, or 3) liberationist or historical-action oriented (Tracy 1981:ch 9). Manifestation theology (Rahner, von Balthasar, Tillich) is most typified by the more Catholic traditions with their rich symbolisms that disclose religious reality and call forth ritual experiences. Proclamation theology (Luther, Barth, Bultmann) emerges from Protestant traditions with an emphasis on prophetic witness to a faith that liberates from all works-righteousness and self-justification. Historical-action theology has transcended denominational boundaries in the works of the Niebuhrs, the social-gospel theologians, and the liberation theologians, who place Christianity before the judgment of both history and the God of justice.

My own experience of the new religious movements has been that, true to their power to revitalize, they find resonance in all three theological methods. Being deeply cultural in origin and purpose, they employ symbolism that discloses the passion of primal religious experience. Because they proclaim reform of life and eschatological purity as well as repentance and ecclesial reform to the missionary churches, they call forth the response of prophetic faith. And with the clear message of social and cultural reform that they set before the eyes of governments, they are authentic loci of liberation praxis.

Carl F. Starkloff, S. J.

As the reflecting church dialogues with these dissenting members, all the above theological methodologies must be operative. Such a development challenges all of us to undertake more than sketches such as I propose here. But the mustard seed is being planted.

NOTES

1. Any theologian of mission will be wise to consider the developmental theology of a salvation to be found in the writings of Irenaeus. Such a "retrieval" would be of great value to future missiology.

2. The work of the Lonerganian scholars is important for any foundational work here. See Bernard J. F. Lonergan (1972) and Robert M. Doran (1981).

3. See Frederick E. Crowe, S. J. (1983:153-69; 1984). These articles are direct references to Lonergan's thought. The brevity of the essay does not permit further development here.

4. My statements here summarize, in part, chapter 3 of Gibson Winter (1981).

REFERENCES

Abbot, Walter M., ed.
    1966   "Declaration of the Relationship of the Church to Non-Christian Religions." *The Documents of Vatican II*. New York: Guild Press.

Crowe, Frederick E., S.J.
    1983   "Son and Spirit: Tension in the Divine Missions?" *Science et Espirit*, 38.
    1984   "Son of God, Holy Spirit, and the World Religions: Lecture on the Contribution of Bernard Lonergan to the Wider Ecumenism," Chancellor's Lecture, Regis College Convocation, November.

Doran, Robert M.
    1981   *Psychic Conversion and Theological Foundations: Toward a Reorientation of the Human Sciences*. Chico, Calif.: Scholars Press.

Eliade, Mircea
    1961   *The Sacred and the Profane*, trans. by Willard R. Trask. New York: Harper and Row.

Carl F. Starkloff, S. J.

1967   *Patterns in Comparative Religion*, trans. by Rosemary
        Sheed. Cleveland: World.

Khodr, Georges
1981   "The Economy of the Holy Spirit," *Mission Trends, No.
        5*, ed. by Gerald H. Anderson and Thomas F. Stransky.
        Ramsey, N.J.: Paulist Press and Grand Rapids:
        Eerdmans.

Kraft, Charles H.
1978   *Christianity in Culture*. Maryknoll: Orbis.

Lonergan, Bernard J. F., S.J.
1972   *Method in Theology*. New York: Herder and Herder.

de Lubac, Henri
1967   *The Mystery of the Supernatural*, trans. by Rosemary
        Sheed. New York: Herder and Herder.

Missiology: An International Review
1985   "New Primal Religious Movements," *Missiology* 13(1).

Niebuhr, H. Richard
1951   *Christ and Culture*. New York: Harper and Row.

Otto, Rudolph
1967   *The Idea of the Holy*, trans. by John W. Harvey. New
        York: Oxford University Press.

Rahner, Karl
1965   "Concerning the Relationship Between Nature and
        Grace," *Theological Investigations*, trans. by Cornelius
        Ernst, O.P. Baltimore: Helicon Press.
1982   *Foundations of Christian Faith*, trans. by William V.
        Dych. New York: Crossroad.

Schlette, Heinz Robert
1966   *Towards a Theology of Religions*. New York: Herder and
        Herder.

Schreiter, Robert J.
1985   *Constructing Local Theologies*. Maryknoll: Orbis.

Segundo, Juan Luis
1973   *The Community Called Church*, trans. by John Drury.
        Maryknoll: Orbis.

Starkloff, Carl F.
1985   "Religious Renewal in Native North America: The Con-
        temporary Call to Mission," *Missiology* 13(1).

Tillich, Paul
    1948,   *The Protestant Era*. Chicago: University of Chicago
    1966   Press.
Tracy, David
    1981   *The Analogical Imagination*. New York: Crossroad.
Turner, Harold W.
    1981   "Religious Movements in Primal (or Tribal) Societies,"
                Mission Focus 9(3).
Van der Leeuw, G.
    1963   *Religion in Essence and Manifestation*, 2 vols., trans. by
                J. E. Turner. New York: Harper and Row.
Wach, Joachim
    1966   *The Comparative Study of Religions*. New York:
                Columbia University.
Winter, Gibson
    1981   "Symbol and Interpretation," *Liberating Creation:*
                Foundations of Religious Social Ethics. New York: Cross-
                road.

Carl F. Starkloff, S. J.

Wilbert R. Shenk
Mennonite Board of Missions

The contribution of the study of new religious movements to missiology

Introduction
According to John G. Gager,

> A curious irony emerges from the titles of two important works in the field of social anthropology. Peter Worsley entitles his study of cargo cults in Melanesia, *The Trumpet Shall Sound*, and Kenelm Burridge's work on millenarian activities bears the title, *New Heaven, New Earth*. Both titles are direct quotations from the New Testament, yet neither author mentions early Christianity except in passing. Indeed, one searches the abundant literature on millenarian movements almost in vain in an effort to ascertain whether anthropologists regard early Christianity as fully, substantially, or tangentially related to millenarian activities in more exotic parts of the world (Gager 1975:20).

A similarly curious irony is found when one sets out to establish a connection between the study of new religious movements and missiology. There is but scant recognition by one field of the other. Our purpose here is to explore this relationship and suggest ways missiological studies might be enriched through closer attention to the study of new religious movements.

Religious studies have flourished during the past two decades. Just as the final triumph of secularization and secularism seemed assured, scholars began noticing religious stirrings which suggested surprising new vitality. To be sure, certain varieties of Christian faith--or of Judaism, or Islam, for that matter--seemed to be losing out, but these were usually more than offset by movements of

179

renewal and innovation which were releasing new energies within the community. Furthermore, new religious movements of immense variety were emerging. Such empirical evidence pointed to a future in which religion would continue to play a vital role.

This unexpected turn is now forcing a reappraisal within the religious studies field. But scholars seem ill-prepared to cope with the new opportunity. Phillip E. Hammond has noted that the scientific study of religion has remained tied to the theoretical constructs of the founders. In the thought of Marx, James, Durkheim, Weber, Freud, Malinowski, and H. R. Niebuhr secularization was assumed to be inevitable and normative. Hammond argues that the time has come to reexamine this model in light of the new data and its apparent inadequacy (Hammond 1985:1-6).

Today we are confronted with an almost embarrassing wealth of materials for the study of all varieties of religious phenomena worldwide. But there are major problems to be resolved. The reductionism which has characterized the "scientific" study of religion is one of these issues. Walter H. Capps has called on religious studies "to develop the methodological apparatus to trace, discern, and understand new religion" (Capps 1978:101; cf. Hargrove 1978:257-66). Without new models and more adequate methods, the new data will be forced through the old grid resulting in the same unsatisfactory results.

Missiology has experienced a similar sort of lag in theoretical development. The theoretical foundations laid by Anderson, Venn, Speer, Allen, Warneck, and Schmidlin in the nineteenth and early twentieth centuries remain largely intact. In spite of a steady flow of critical studies of the philosophy and methodology characteristic of missionary work since 1800, and notwithstanding calls for new paradigms, we are still dependent on that original inheritance.[1]

Missiological studies have exhibited ambivalence both toward religious studies and new religious movements, and that with some reason. The missiologist has generally felt the suspicion of colleagues in the social sciences and religious studies over the supposed lack of scientific rigor, objectivity, and detachment from the matter under study. Whether this implied criticism was justified is not our question at the moment.

Missiologists have fared little better in relation to new religious movements. A perusal of the standard missiological journals turns up relatively few articles on this theme; equally few books have been published. Yet missionaries and scholars closely related to the missionary movement have been among the pioneers in the field. Generally, their point of departure has been to produce an objective scholarly study working within the confines of an academic discipline. It is worth noting several scholars who are exceptions to this rule by virtue of their attempts to build bridges between disciplines.

David J. Hesselgrave edited a volume, *Dynamic Religious Movements* (1978), which presented twelve case studies of rapidly growing religious movements from various parts of the world. As Hesselgrave points out in his introduction, the writers kept essentially one question in mind: why is this movement growing? Other critical questions were bracketed.

Hesselgrave had a clear missiological objective. He was suing for the attention of those concerned about the mission of the church and challenging them to think about processes of growth by learning from religious movements which were gaining adherents, regardless of whether these were counted in Christian ranks or not.

A quite different, pioneering effort is Gottfried Oosterwal's theological critique of what he called *Modern Messianic Movements* (1973). Oosterwal demonstrated great appreciation for the movements he studied which he had known firsthand in the field. He urged the wider Christian community to appreciate the authenticity of the quest in which many of these groups were engaged. But he also pointed to questionable elements which had to be judged by a Christological norm. He underscored the importance of a missiological approach which took full account of the eschatological dimension--the dimension which all too often had been lacking or distorted in the missionary message but which these movements were poised to hear.

No one has seen the relationship between new religious movements and missiology more clearly nor worked with greater perseverance to get the attention of the missiological community than has Harold W. Turner.[2] Combining appreciation for these movements with an understanding of the phenomenon worldwide and its manifold interfaces with the historical Christian churches, Turner has attempted to lay on the conscience of the Christian community its responsibility to come to terms with the complex features of Modern Missions which exerted far-reaching positive influence as well as pursuing some policies, practices, and attitudes which proved to be counter-productive (cf. Turner 1973:47-65; 1984:111-13). He also urged new openness to relate to these movements missiologically. Turner has continually worked to contribute to scholarly understanding of these movements by demonstrating their importance to the fields of the history and phenomenology of religion, on the one hand, while being concerned for the human rights of the adherents on the other.

Missiology

Missiology is both old and relatively new. In his survey of the development of missiology as a discipline, Johannes Verkuyl demonstrates that though there was some awareness of the need for formal study of missionary action early in the nineteenth century, it was not welcomed and given a place until the twentieth century (Verkuyl 1978:ch.1). Despite advocacy by prominent mission leaders, it long was a sickly plant which had difficulty striking root. The mission agencies invested scant resources in the formal study of the "science of missions," as it was called in the nineteenth century. When they did sponsor missionary training institutions, they insisted on emphasizing the practical aspects since theory was considered to be largely irrelevant.

But it was equally difficult to find a place for mission studies in the academy. This difficulty stemmed from causes both internal and external. This period was not noteworthy for its theological productivity. Furthermore, ideas about the theological curriculum were rather fixed. Innovation was resisted. Externally, the influence of the Enlightenment continued to work its way into all areas of life. As Martin E. Marty has demonstrated, several "paths to the secular" were taken--he draws contrasting portraits of the Continental, British, and American experiences--but the long-term effect was diminished influence for religion in public life and cultural development (Marty 1969). Toward the end of the century a few intrepid figures such as Gustav Warneck in Germany managed to win a toehold for the academic study of missions.

Thus, missiology as a discipline suffered from this double bind. It was largely held at arm's length by the practical-minded missionary societies and it was only grudgingly granted a place on the margin of the theological faculty in the university.

Verkuyl offers a multifaceted definition of missiology, reflecting to some degree its hybrid character as a discipline:

> Missiology is the study of the salvation activities of the Father, Son, and Holy Spirit throughout the world geared toward bringing the kingdom of God into existence. . .[It is] the study of the world-wide church's divine mandate to be ready to serve this God who is aiming his saving acts toward this world. Missiology's task in every age is to investigate scientifically and critically the presuppositions, motives, structures, methods, patterns of cooperation and leadership which the churches bring to their mandate (Verkuyl 1978:5).

Such an enterprise requires various tools and involves intersections with several disciplines, including the science of religion. According to Verkuyl: "Without a phenomenology of and history of the current religions, proper dialogue with and missionary approach to these religions are impossible" (Verkuyl 1978:10). It should be noted, however, that Verkuyl here has in mind the major religions of the world. New religious movements do not come within his purview.

To recapitulate, a functional definition of missiology includes the following features:

1. History of the Christian movement, especially its expansion;
2. Normative content, foundation, and motivation for Christian mission;
3. Contemporary situation which shapes present context;
4. Trends which will influence the future.

The discipline of missiology then will draw on biblical and theological studies, church history, and the human sciences.

New religious movements and missions

The phenomenon of new religious movements usually is divided into two major groupings. The first includes movements in the industrialized Western world. These are movements which generally have appeared since 1945. The second group is comprised of movements which have sprung into existence outside the West. These movements are the product of the encounter between a powerful external influence and a primal society. In general, new religious movements arise as a result of upheaval and clash. But the one variety occurs primarily intraculturally while the other results from intercultural contacts.

Little attention has been paid to the interface between these two groups or to what they have in common vis-à-vis culture change. The fact of the persistence of religion worldwide--and indeed its vitality and intensity of innovation--puts a new set of questions to all students of religion. Earlier theories about the future of religion in the face of secularization have fallen along the way. These new movements seem to reaffirm that religion requires a certain intensity of experience if it is to shape values and compel loyalty.[3]

One of the key observations students of new religious movements in primal societies have made is that the emergence of these movements can be correlated with the presence of Christian missions. In his study of this phenomenon in Africa David Barrett asserted,

> "It is in fact the case that schisms from foreign mission bodies in Africa have been taking place for the last hundred years on a scale unparalleled in the entire history of the expansion of Christianity. . . . Most of these movements have emerged spontaneously in areas that have been subjected with intensity to Christian missionary activity for several decades" (Barrett 1968:3)

Numerous studies can be cited to substantiate Barrett's contention.

Our purpose here simply is to establish the genetic link between the missionary movement and the emergence of new religious movements in primal societies worldwide. As Turner argued in his 1973 article on the situation of the North American Indians, this fact ought at least to force missiologists to begin asking what was the flaw in a missionary approach which produced these deleterious results (Turner 1973:62). We should be able to ask these critical questions without condemning wholesale everything done in the past or failing to understand the scale of achievement of the modern missionary movement since 1800.

It appears it would be fruitful indeed to pursue an investigation into a theme which relates directly to a specific Christian initiative carried out over a long historical period in diverse circumstances which has produced widely a quite unintended result. Even at this late date such playback would be valuable. Several benefits might accrue from such scrutiny.

A generation ago Max Warren drew on Martin Buber's concept of "I and Thou" to develop a theology of relationship and attention for "real life is meeting." If we study these groups which are reactions to the coming of Western missions, we will see mirrored in them the mission project sponsored from the West. In other words, people of the West will see themselves, both their strengths and foibles, through the eyes of others. It will also open up new vistas on peoples who have both selectively appropriated from the Christian revelation and rejected parts of historical Christianity as represented by the West. In other words, the act of reverent and sympathetic study can open the way for "meeting."

Another benefit would be the challenge to greater integrity in the message. Jean Guiart and Mircea Eliade were of one mind in asserting that missionaries in the South Pacific failed to comprehend the fullness of the Christian faith and consequently did not appreciate the responses of the indigenous peoples. In other words, the Melanesians could hear authentic notes in the Christian faith to which the missionaries, conditioned by Western culture, were tone deaf. Primitive Christianity was millenial, a theme which the missionaries could not successfully suppress in their preaching. The Melanesians were especially sensitive to this motif and interpreted much of what they heard and saw demonstrated by the missionaries as being an earnest of what was yet to come. In their historical situation they felt themselves to be a victim people and yearned for liberation from oppression and injustice. They heard in the gospel a promise of release and a new life of peace and prosperity. The irony was that the missionaries shared many of these perspectives but the vocabulary they used to get their agenda across failed to communicate to the local peoples (Guiart and Eliade 1970:122-43). Ultimately, disillusionment set in as these millenial expectations were not fulfilled; and cargo-cults emerged.

A genuine "meeting" would have opened the way for a more reciprocal sharing of the message, with the missionaries understanding why the Melanesians were attracted by the millenial theme and the Melanesians being given opportunity to hear why to the missionaries other accents were important.

Wilbert R. Shenk

Salient features of new religious movements

Essentially, the charge that has been brought against the modern missionary movement is that it was but another attempt to universalize something which was profoundly particular and parochial, namely Western civilization. And this is experienced as the ultimate effrontery: one culture or people arrogate to themselves the role of determining and managing the destinies of other peoples.

None of this is new, of course; it has been attempted repeatedly throughout history in both religious and political terms. The early Christian church faced such a situation. The party of "Judaizers" wanted to insist to Gentile believers that they accept the Jewish law as a condition for their admittance into the Christian family. This conflict led to the conference held in Jerusalem reported in Acts 15. That conference decision affirmed the validity of both Jewish and Gentile cultures but declared that neither had salvific significance; neither was to be elevated to the level of a universal determinant binding on all people everywhere.

The situations of the early church and the modern missionary movement differ in important ways, however. The early church comprised a community which was socially marginal and powerless. The modern mission movement has long been viewed by critics as simply the religious dimension of a massive and powerful Western movement to colonize and dominate the world. The early Christians were numbered among the persecuted and suffering while Western Christianity has been seen as the religion of the powerful. To some extent this is an unfair caricature. But there are lessons to be learned as well.

Missiology itself evolved as a tool to rationalize and make more efficient the Christianizing process. One can find among the pioneer missiologists those who developed critical perspectives on missionary methods and policies. And there are shining examples of missionaries who were keenly aware of the social or political plight of the people among whom they were living and sided with them in their struggle for justice. But pragmatism was the keynote of missionary thought and practice.

In the first part we have argued that missiology does indeed need the contribution which a study of new religious movements in primal societies could make, especially those movements which identify themselves as being in some sense Christian, since these groups have emerged in response to Western missions.

We turn now to an exploration of six facets of that contribution: contextualization, theological reformulation, religious innovation, economic and cultural development, church growth, and ecumenical relationships. The opportunity before missiology is to become the science of the *oikoumene* in the service of the *missio Dei*, on behalf of the whole body, for the salvation of the world. A respectful listening to and learning from these movements will foster development of a more self-critical and positive missiology.

Precursors to contextualization

From its earliest days the modern missionary movement was marked by a confusion of perspective. On the one hand, mission promoters frequently depicted the task to be done as a fairly simple matter of presenting the Christian message in a straightforward manner to peoples sunk in despair and, who, consequently, would respond gladly and quickly. On the other side was the growing group of missionaries in the field who knew firsthand how complicated the process was. As foreigners they had to master a strange language--often before it was written--and try to understand a highly intricate culture with quite another worldview. Learning the new language and culture were prerequisite to any effective communication of the Christian message. As the complexity of the task became more apparent, mission theorists moved through several stages as they sought to conceptualize the task.

The great theoretical breakthrough in missions thought in the nineteenth century was identification of the "indigenous church" as the goal of mission. This was particularly important to Protestants. Other theoretical and policy developments were largely an embroidering on this basic theme.

Prior to the enunciation of this principle around 1850, missions were conceived as an act of carrying out Christ's last command. A variety of motives were invoked to stir the faithful to give and to go. But the introduction of the indigenous church as goal of mission offered what seemed to be a coherent and measurable goal toward which missionary efforts could be directed. Mission societies developed elaborate strategies and policies to achieve this goal. This concept continued to be the linchpin of mission thought for the next 100 years.

Notwithstanding the theoretical tidiness of the "indigenous church" concept, it became evident early on that missionary practice fell short of the ideal. A cursory review of the literature shows that periodically books were published which criticized the approach missions were taking and a restatement of the indigenous church ideal was made. For example, John L. Nevius wrote a series of articles for the *Chinese Recorder* in 1885, later issued in book form, which set forth his alternative to the deformed missionary practice he saw around him. Roland Allen first gained notice in 1912 with his book, *Missionary Methods: St. Paul's or Ours?*, a stern attack on contemporary missions. Other similar works followed. The World Dominion movement emerged in the 1920s as gadfly to missions, with its central concern being to encourage the development of indigenous churches.[4]

The political climate was undergoing important change throughout this period. Nationalist movements were springing to life in all of the countries colonized by the European powers. Frequently Christians joined their compatriots in these movements for political independence.

In *The Philosophy of the Christian World Mission* published in 1943, Edmund D. Soper asked: "Has Christianity demonstrated in the modern world, as it did in the two previous periods of achievement, that it can be a part of the life of all kinds of people, differing in race, nationality, and location? . . . Can Christianity become truly 'indigenous' to the culture and life of a people?" (p. 125). Later Soper notes: "At the present time indigenization is a most pressing matter. Just as there is a British, a German, and an American type of Christianity, so there is a demand that the Christianity of Japan be distinctively Japanese . . ." (Soper 1943:266). Soper demonstrated the importance of expressing the Christian faith through the art forms, architecture, and cultural customs of a people rather than with what is imported.

At about the same time another movement was being launched which was to promote the application of cultural anthropology to missionary work and Bible translation. Through the creative leadership of scholars such as Eugene A. Nida this movement quickly gained influence. Books continued to be produced during the 1940s and 1950s expounding the "indigenous church" theme. John Ritchie published *Indigenous Church Principles in Theory and Practice in 1946.*[5] A Pentecostal missionary administrator, Melvin L. Hodges, wrote a little book in 1953 entitled *The Indigenous Church.* This book enjoyed wide influence. It is primarily a restatement of the classical nineteenth century "three-selfs" formula, but it shows no historical awareness and the influence of the newly emerging missionary anthropology is conspicuously absent. T. S. Soltau's *Missions at the Crossroads* appeared the following year (1954). Soltau had served in Korea where the Nevius Plan had been implemented effectively. He advocated "the indigenous church" as "a solution for the unfinished task."

Several threads run through the literature from Nevius to Soltau. First, there is an implicit critique of contemporary mission practice in its failure to live up to the ideal. Second, despite disclaimers along the way, the controlling assumption is that the outcome depends largely on mission leadership. Third, there is virtually no conceptual development during these six decades. Essentially the same patterns and programs are advocated in 1954 as in 1900. In other words, the blueprint has been little altered. Fourth, insights from indigenous cultures are not appropriated in the service of more incisive analysis. The focus seems to be obsessively set on mission structure and administration. Fifth, despite the implicit critique of mission practice, the closest anyone came to a thorough-going evaluation was Roland Allen. And he stirred deeply negative reactions so that his insights were not widely appreciated and applied.

Viewed in the perspective of the foregoing summary, William A. Smalley's brief critique of the "indigenous church" in *Practical Anthropology* in 1958 takes on added importance as a harbinger of what was to come. He pointed out that the three-selfs were quite inadequate as diagnostic tools. He suggested "that the three 'selfs' are really projections of our American value system into the idealization of the church" (Smalley 1958:51-65). He sketched out a more dynamic and creative role for the missionary as a source of cultural alternatives to aid the new church in making choices.

Undoubtedly, the contribution of the cultural anthropologists found ready acceptance both for its fresh insights and new tools and

Wilbert R. Shenk

because of the influential writings of Stephen Neill, Max Warren, Walter Freytag and others who put the state of the mission movement in the broad historical and theological perspective. The International Missionary Council played a key role in organizing conferences around timely themes which encouraged lively debate and continuing missiological ferment.

The next decade was a time of identity crisis for missions culminating around 1970 in the call for a moratorium on the sending of missionaries from the West to other parts of the world. This demand by the younger churches for full autonomy coincided with the granting of political independence to virtually all colonial possessions by the European powers.

The year 1972 marks an important shift in theory. A new term which quickly superseded "indigenous" was introduced into the lexicon of missiology. The term "contextualization," in spite of its linguistic gracelessness, changed the angle of vision on a whole range of issues. Fundamental to all else, however, was the way it shifted the locus of attention to the host culture. It built on the notion--by now widely accepted--that every culture can be a vehicle for the gospel. In contrast to the theory of the indigenous church, for which no theological foundation was ever developed, proponents of contextualization appealed to the incarnation as fundamental to missionary witness.

While Protestant missions from the beginning emphasized the importance of translating the Scriptures into the vernacular languages, Roman Catholic practice adhered to another tradition which kept the Bible locked up in a holy language. In this regard, Vatican Council II signaled an important shift by approving the use of vernacular languages for worship and encouraged the use of Scriptures by all members of the church. For both Roman Catholics and Protestants the introduction of the concept of contextualization offered a new theoretical construct for understanding the communication of the Christian message, as well as a framework for evaluating the effectiveness of missionary practice.

Although new religious movements--frequently called independent churches but encompassing a range wider than this term implies--began emerging more than a century ago wherever missions went, few people asked what these movements might have to teach.[6]

One of the outstanding features of new religious movements was, of course, their indigenous character. By definition, these groups emerged out of a particular culture with all its distinctive features and idiom. And they were not dependent on external sources for financial support or leadership.

These groups have typically arisen in response to a crisis experience of an individual or group indigenous to that culture. Frequently, a charismatic leader has appeared as a catalytic agent bringing about resolution in a time of crisis in ways culturally appropriate to that group.

That is not to say that a new group accepts only those elements and materials indigenous to their own group. A movement may borrow and adapt elements from various sources but ultimately the outcome is one suitable to and understood by the people of that culture. Thus, the result rings true in that place and time.

For example, the Church of the Lord (Aladura) in Nigeria adopted a liturgical structure which superficially reflects the Anglican tradition out of which the founder and first members came. But the way it has been incorporated into the Church of the Lord (Aladura) worship has given it a Yoruba flavor and style.

Furthermore, the theological agenda of these new religious movements indicates that it is genuinely theirs rather than that of an outsider. They are free to emphasize those themes most important to them in worship--joyous spontaneity, the use of indigenous musical instruments and forms--and to give a different balance to the Christian message than would be typical in the West. For example, many of these movements give priority to healing, deliverance from evil powers, and prayer.

Thus, long before the term contextualization came into vogue in missiological circles, these new religious movements were living laboratories of that which had to come about if the churches in the non-Western world were to take root and survive. Because these movements had arisen outside the control of Western influences, they exhibited a contextualized religious response to what they had heard in the Christian message from the outset.

Wilbert R. Shenk

The re-visioning of theology

With the passage of time it became increasingly clear that failure of the church to find rootage in Asian, African, or Latin American soil--i.e., the failure of the indigenous church program--was due, in no small measure, to the very nature of Western theology. Theology was no more exempt from cultural peculiarities than liturgy, architecture, clerical raiment, or what constituted social gentility.

In the 1950s K. A. Busia, later prime minister of Ghana, asserted: "For the conversion to the Christian faith to be more than superficial, the Christian Church must come to grips with traditional beliefs and practices, and with the world view that these beliefs and practices imply" (Baëta, 1971:20). A decade later another well-known African scholar, Bolaji Idowu, charged: "The Church in Africa came into being with prefabricated theology, liturgies, and traditions. In the matter of Christian ethics, the converts found themselves in the position of those early converts before the Council of Jerusalem (Acts 15)" (Idowu 1968:426). Idowu had already made these same points with eloquence and conviction in a little book, *Towards an Indigenous Church* (1965). Both Busia and Idowu called for a deepened appreciation of indigenous culture and a theology adapted to the pastoral needs of their peoples.

Busia and Idowu stood in a long line of leaders who saw the need for a fresh understanding of theology if the new church was to be given the help needed in fully appropriating the faith. For example, Hendrik Kraemer and J. H. Bavinck advocated the reformulation of theological education in Indonesia in the 1920s in order that young seminarians might study theologia in loco. It appears that Kraemer and Bavinck at that time were voices crying in the wilderness. Books written during the period on "indigenous church principles" emphasized the importance of thorough training for church leaders but it was assumed that such training would be Western (cf. Rowland 1925:147-56).

By the late 1960s it was increasingly understood that how theology is conceived and transmitted powerfully shapes a church with the potential either of making it exotic or indigenous. Soon one began to hear about all sorts of theologies and the quest for indigenous theologies quickly gained momentum. John S. Mbiti conceived of the task as that of holding in tension the universal kerygma and many provincial theologies (Mbiti 1976:6).

Mbiti suggested that genuine theology could emerge only out of deep experience. The mission-founded churches had been inhibited from serious theological engagement with their own cultures by an over-protectiveness on the part of the missions. The result was retarded development. Thus Mbiti looked for an alternative source. He regarded the independent churches as "ultimately an expression of theological protest" even though they were not the direct result of church-mission controversies (Mbiti 1976:16). In their "protest" they had developed authentic African responses to the gospel.

What approach should be taken in developing theologies in context? E. W. Fasholé-Luke has suggested that a theology for Africa be developed by tapping four sources: the Bible, traditional religions and philosophy, the Western theological inheritance, and the experience of the independent churches (Fasholé-Luke, 1976:141-44). Although the latter typically do not have a formal written theology, they have dressed important biblical themes in African garb and have freely danced and sung of their faith in Jesus Christ.

Indeed, it is precisely this nonformal style which has raised questions about what constitutes theology. Is a faith tradition built and nurtured through the traditional pedagogy of recital any less authentic? Can not theology shaped through encounter with spiritual forces in prayer and pastoral ministry have an integrity of its own?

The question of how theology develops may well turn out to have quite another answer when the culture under consideration is oral (cf. Hollenweger 1980:68-75). In oral societies the collective memory is stored in stories and songs and regularly relived. It is quite wrong to impose artificially on such a society an approach to theology which demands tomes of systematic theology written in a foreign language for a totally different people in another period of history.

In an important study of the contribution of independent churches in Africa to the development of an African theology, M. L. Daneel pays particular attention to Christology (Daneel 1984:76-88; cf. Bediako 1983:81-113). Despite a lack of written theological reflections, one can discern in their lived experience and biographies of leaders a vital awareness of the suffering Christ who has transformed life. "A study of the historic development of the Independent

Wilbert R. Shenk

Churches illuminates the change from 'oppressive suffering' to 'redemptive suffering' " (Daneel 1984:80). As did Jesus, these disciples have identified with the oppressed, resisted the oppressor, and preached hope.

But Christ the Victor also plays an important role in dealing with the powers and in healing. The independent churches have understood the work of Jesus through the paradigm of the traditional healers. In drawing on the familiar they have also transformed it by attributing the insight which comes to them in diagnosing illnesses to the presence of the Holy Spirit. These churches also recognize the lordship of Christ in cultivating among their members an awareness of the divine presence in worship and especially during the Eucharist. But Jesus also commissions his followers to go out as ambassadors (Daneel 1984:86ff,; cf. 1980:105-20).

Through the study of the religious movements we gain further perspective on this fundamental fact. Each movement produces a formal structure of belief, doctrine, or creed. Typically few of them have elaborate frameworks, and fewer still have even begun to produce a systematic theology. But each has a self-conscious thought structure.

The structures or patterns are identifiably the product of the culture of origin and represents the response to that context. This development, as depicted in new religious movements, demonstrates that theology must be dynamically contextual. This means that theology may be constructed in modes other than Hellenistic philosophical categories. Furthermore, it suggests that orthopraxy is certainly as important, especially among pre-literate peoples as orthodoxy. And it suggests that theology is a dynamic, living, growing interpretation of the faith in response to a changing environment. If it fails to respond to that environment, it will become irrelevant.

The way we think about theology today in the West has been directly affected by the experiences of churches in the non-Western world. And that experience has been influenced by the examples of the new religious movements.

Primal societies as seedbed for religious innovation

It has been recognized for some time that new adherents to the Christian faith, following the initial Jewish phase, have been won

194

almost exclusively among primal societies rather than among other major religions of the world. New religious movements furnish several lessons concerning this fact.

The peoples of primal societies are highly vulnerable in the face of stronger and dominating cultures. The peoples of primal societies seemingly are easily overwhelmed by the stronger cultures. Representatives of Western cultures in particular have tended to treat these primal societies as inferior and to patronize them by offering the supposed benefits of "civilization." Westerners have failed to respect them by prescribing rapid acculturation to Western culture as the path to modernization.

But the primal culture has proved to be amazingly persistent. Forced acculturation has usually done nothing more than push primal features underground. These then re-emerge in times of crisis, often in quite unexpected forms. Indeed, we can find abundant examples of such resurgence of primal religiosity in the West as well. The flowering of witchcraft and magic in nineteenth-century France, in the face of a national program of secularization, is but one example.[7]

The study of new religious movements in recent years has demonstrated the importance of taking seriously and understanding sympathetically these primal forms as a prerequisite to knowing religious reality in any society. Any such study will force us to ask in relation to a given culture what is the meaning of conversion? It will require us to inquire as to the nature of religiosity of a particular people. It calls us to come to terms with the worldview of which this religiosity is an expression.

Religion as ally of cultural change and development

At one time in the West, hundreds of years ago, religion was considered indispensable to civilization for it was the source of cultural innovation and anchor for all of life. Beginning with the Renaissance, religion in the West began to lose this special status. From the Enlightenment onward, religion came into disrepute. It was characterized as being reactionary and an impediment to social progress. Marxist theoreticians and many scientists have seen religion as being a drag on human advancement.

Wilbert R. Shenk

The period since 1945 has been marked both by the gaining of political independence by former colonies of the European powers and a concerted effort to modernize the less developed nations. The development movement has been dominated by rational planning, the application of scientific technology, and major infusions of capital. The development literature is notable for its disdain for religion. This attitude is reflected both in the dismissive attitude assumed by most development experts toward religion and the meager amount of literature devoted to the religion-development nexus. Even in Christian circles little has been done to challenge this highly tendentious attitude (von der Mehden 1986: esp. ch. 1).

The Swedish economist Gunnar Myrdal concluded from his massive three-volume study, *Asian Drama* (1968), that the major obstacles Asian nations faced in their development efforts lay in the realm of values and worldview rather than in the organizational and technical spheres. Two decades later it is increasingly acknowledged that religion is indeed a vital force--both positive and negative--in national development which cannot be ignored.

The new religious movements have been cheerfully unaware of these strictures against religion. On the contrary, new religious movements have turned to religion as a source of development and change.

They have done this, first of all, by drawing instinctively from religion those values which are prerequisite to progress. Many of these groups, for example, have insisted on an ethic of self- restraint and thrift. They have prized personal discipline and integrity. They have taught their adherents to be industrious and set goals. By offering their people liberation from evil powers, they have desacralized the material and political world. In addition, these groups frequently encouraged a spirit of self-determination and self-responsibility. All of these are significant components in human development (Turner 1980:523-33; 1982).

These movements have been important in another way. In numerous cases, they have fostered new forms of social organization which helped their followers to cope with dysfunctional aspects of their former way of life. The Aiyetoro community in Nigeria adopted a communitarian form of organization which for a period of time enabled members of the community to reach a new level of productivity and well-being. The Korsten basket weavers of Zambia represent another case where a marginal group of people organized themselves into an effective economic unit which benefited all its members.

From the beginning of the modern missionary movement it was assumed that there was an intimate connection between the Christian message and personal and social development. Symbolically the capstone of this understanding was the large three-volume report by James S. Dennis, *Christian Missions and Social Progress*, published at the turn of the twentieth century. This is a veritable catalog of all the changes wrought in non-Western lands through the influence of Christian missions. Dennis' work appeared during the period when the Social Gospel movement was coming into its own. World War I shattered much of that optimism, and missions went on the defensive as the nationalist movements gained momentum. Thus the attitude shifted from one extreme to another. A respectful study of new religious movements will help restore a more balanced view of the role of religion in human development. Missiology may once more have a positive contribution to make in this field.

Basis for understanding processes of church growth

At the beginning of this essay we noted the role which power played in the movement of Western peoples to other parts of the world. Christian missions have also been stamped by the various forms of power on which they depended in the carrying out of the mission. What we have failed to understand or acknowledge is the impact this has had on mission-founded churches, their relationship to the missions, and those groups which arose in reaction to but independently of the missions. This needs to be understood both in terms of historical process as well as relationships. This can be visualized in terms of a dialectic moving from thesis to antithesis and then synthesis.

1. **Thesis**. At this stage the Western mission enters the scene bringing several things. The mission obviously offers a new religious message. In addition, the mission advocates an alternative worldview. But the mission also represents a dominant culture which demands submission to it. In the course of time a church is formed but one which is tied to the mission and the church which sent it.

This involves the rejection by the new adherents of their own culture at a deep and crucial point, namely value system, family loyalties, communal solidarity. The result is an alienation between the new adherents and their own people.

2. **Antithesis.** At some point a reaction to the initial stage sets in. The reaction may be encouraged by a nationalist political movement or in some other more religious form. But at the heart of the reaction is a rejection of "mission" Christianity. The people may continue to cling to the kernel of the Christian message but seek to throw off the husk in which it was brought to them.

One way of dealing with such a situation is to call for a moratorium in an effort to break the pattern and system by which outside power has controlled the development of the church.

New religious movements have, of course, had complete autonomy from such outside influences by virtue of their spontaneous emergence. They are nonetheless also an antithetical statement about "mission" Christianity.

3. **Synthesis.** A resolution to the preceding stage can come only when there is a synthesis opening the way to the establishment of new relationships based on equality and even interdependence. The weakness of the classical "indigenous church" ideal was that it suggested that the ultimate stage for the new church was achieved when it had absolute autonomy and no longer looked to the mission for relationship. Both theologically and sociologically this is untenable. The church has come into being precisely through this outside influence and the relationship cannot be denied. Once the dysfunctional elements in that relationship have been corrected, both on the part of the dominant mission and the subservient church, a satisfying partnership can be effected.

A mature relationship will recognize the integrity of both parties and their mutual need of one another. A part of that acceptance will involve recognition by the mission of the strength of a theology and liturgy which are more thoroughly contextual and appreciation for the way in which this contextuality can become a gift to the church universal.

Thus the study of new religious movements can provide an alternative model for understanding how the church grows. Churches which have never experienced a period of mission tutelage have less need to be reactionary and are more spontaneously indigenous in their faith expression. But they also frequently suffer lacks--interaction with other Christian traditions both contemporary and historical, access to the Scriptures and leadership training, a sense of acceptance by the wider Christian community.

Ecumenical challenge

The act of studying new religious movements, if carried out in a sympathetic, sensitive, and appreciative attitude, is a first step in ecumenical recognition of the validity of new forms of Christian life. Interaction with these new religious movements has shown several things. First, those new religious movements with a Christological orientation are usually reaching out for fraternal relationships and seeking to understand their place in the wider Christian history and tradition. Far from rejecting other Christians, they want to understand and be understood.

Second, the ecumenical dimension is not simply a call to relationship. It also implies an acknowledgement that these groups emerging out of the interaction between Western and non-Western forms has produced a new genre of Christian thought and practice which can enrich the life of the church universal.

Third, this is a call for mutual submission. It invites Western Christians to submit their orthodoxies to the scrutiny of the new religious movements. It opens the way for adherents of the new religious movements to submit their orthopraxies to scrutiny in the light of Jesus Christ. Together both Western church and new religious movement will discover what it means to follow Jesus Christ--the one who alone holds all together.

NOTES

1. Cf. inter alia Walbert Buhlmann (1976:383-94), which describes the changing world situation and consequent need for further theoretical development.

2. Several of his essays on this theme have been collected and republished as a section in *Religious Innovation in Africa* (1979:255-93). He was guest editor for the January 1985 issue of *Missiology* with the theme "New Primal Religious Movements."

3. Cf. chapters by Dick Anthony, Thomas Robbins and Paul Schwartz, and John Coleman in *New Religious Movements* (Coleman and Baum 1983:1-16). For a critical overview see Eileen Barker (1985:36-57).

4. Perhaps the best-known pamphlet published by World Dominion was *The Indigenous Church* by Sidney J. W. Clark, which he originally wrote at the request of the National Christian Council of China at the conclusion of an extensive survey of missions in China in 1913.

5. Ritchie was a long-time missionary to Peru who was serving with the American Bible Society when he wrote his book.

6. See the fascinating study by Janet Hodgson (1984:19-33) on a movement going back to 1815. A group of scholars has rejected this interpretation. The book *African Christianity--Patterns of Religious Continuity*, edited by George Bond, Walton Johnson, and Sheila Walker (1979), embodies this alternative approach, rejecting the notion that these movements are a response to a clash between outside influences and indigenous dynamics. Rather they see these African churches as expressions of indigenous forces in continuity with their religious past. A sophisticated analysis and critique of the crisis/response model is that of Robert S. Ellwood, Jr., "Emergent Religion in America: An Historical Perspective" (1978:267-84). Ellwood offers the "emergent" model instead--each emergence arises out of latent religious elements.

7. Cf. Thomas A. Kselman, *Miracles and Prophecies in Nineteenth-Century France*: "It is somewhat puzzling that the forces of 'modernization' seen as producing outbursts of religious enthusiasm in other centuries and cultures are generally seen to have no similar consequences for the nineteenth century. The number, significance, and visibility of miracle cults and prophetic movements in France, with Lourdes as the leading example, suggest that our understanding of France's modernization must be revised" (1983:195). In an older study, *Witchcraft--European and African* (1963), Geoffrey Parrinder sought to demonstrate similarities and continuities between traditional cultures in Africa and Europe.

REFERENCES

Allen, Roland
  1912   *Missionary Methods: St. Paul's or Ours?* London: Robert
          Scott.

Baëta, Christian
  1971   "Some Aspects of Religious Change in Africa," *Ghana
          Bulletin of Theology*, 3(10).

Barker, Eileen
  1985   "New Religious Movements: Yet Another Great
          Awakening?" *The Sacred in a Secular Age*, ed. by Phillip
          E. Hammond, Berkeley, Calif.: University of California
          Press.

Barrett, David B.
  1968   *Schism and Renewal in Africa*. Nairobi, Kenya: Oxford
          University Press.

Bediako, Kwame
  1983   "Biblical Christologies in the Context of African
          Traditional Religions," *Sharing Jesus in the Two-Thirds
          World*, ed. by Vinay Samuel and Chris Sugden. Grand
          Rapids: Eerdmans.

Bond, George, Walton Johnson, and Sheila Walker
  1979   *African Christianity: Patterns of Religious Continuity*. New
          York: Academic Press.

Bosch, David J.
  1983   "An Emerging Paradigm for Missions," *Missiology*,
          11(4).

Buhlmann, Walbert
  1976   *The Coming of the Third Church*. Maryknoll, N.Y.: Orbis
          Books.

Capps, Walter H.
  1978   "The Interpretation of New Religion and Religious
          Studies," *Understand the New Religions*, ed. by Jacob
          Needleman and George Baker. New York: Seabury
          Press.

Clark, Sidney J. W.
  1913   *The Indigenous Church*. World Dominion.

Coleman, John, and Gregory Baum, ed.
  1983   *New Religious Movements*. New York: Seabury Press.

Wilbert R. Shenk

Daneel, M. L.
  1980   "The Missionary Outreach of African Independent
          Churches," *Missionalia*, 8(3).
  1984   "Towards a *Theologia Africana*? The Contribution of
          Independent Churches to African Theology," *Missionalia*, 12(2).
Dennis, James S.
  1897-   *Christian Missions and Social Progress*. New York:
  1906   Revell.
Eliade, Mircea
  1970   " 'Cargo Cults' and Cosmic Regeneration," *Millenial
          Dreams in Action*, ed. by Sylvia L. Thrupp. New York:
          Schocken Books.
Ellwood, Robert S., Jr.
  1978   "Emergent Religion in America: An Historical Perspective," *Understanding the New Religions*, ed. by Jacob
          Needleman and George Baker. New York: Seabury.
Fasholé-Luke, E. W.
  1976   "The Quest for African Christian Theologies," *Mission
          Trends No. 3--Third World Theologies*, ed. by Gerald H.
          Anderson and Thomas F. Stransky. New York/Grand
          Rapids: Paulist/Eerdmans.
Gager, John G.
  1975   *Kingdom and Community: The Social World of Early
          Christianity*. Englewood Cliffs, N.J.: Prentice-Hall.
Guiart, Jean
  1970   "Conversion to Christianity in the South Pacific,"
          Millenial Dreams in Action, ed. by Sylvia L. Thrupp. New
          York: Schocken Books.
Hammond, Phillip E., ed.
  1985   *The Sacred in a Secular Age: Toward Revision in the
          Scientific Study of Religion*. Berkeley, Calif.: University of
          California Press.
Hargrove, Barbara
  1978   "Integrative and Transformative Religions," *Understand
          the New Religions*, ed. by Jacob Needleman and George
          Baker. New York: Seabury Press.

Hesselgrave, David J., ed.
  1978   *Dynamic Religious Movements*. Grand Rapids: Baker Book House.
Hodges, Melvin L.
  1953   *The Indigenous Church*. Springfield, Mo.: Gospel Publishing House (republished in several editions).
Hodgson, Janet
  1984   "Ntsikana--Precursor of Independency," *Missionalia*, 12:(1).
Hollenweger, Walter J.
  1980   "Charismatic Renewal in the Third World: Implications for Mission," *Occasional Bulletin for Missionary Research*, 4(2).
Idowu, E. Bolaji
  1965   *Towards an Indigenous Church*. London/Ibadan: Oxford University Press.
  1968   "The Predicament of the Church in Africa," in C. G. Baëta (ed.), *Christianity in Tropical Africa*. London: Oxford University Press, 417-37.
Kselman, Thomas A.
  1983   *Miracles and Prophecies in Nineteenth-Century France*. New Brunswick, N.J.: Rutgers University Press.
Marty, Martin E.
  1969   *The Modern Schism: Three Paths to the Secular*. New York: Harper and Row.
Mbiti, John S.
  1976   "Theological Impotence and the Universality of the Church," *Mission Trends No. 3--Third World Theologies*, ed. by Gerald H. Anderson and Thomas F. Stransky. New York/Grand Rapids, Mich.: Paulist/Eerdmans.
Mehden, Fred R. von der
  1986   *Religion and Modernization in Southeast Asia*. Syracuse, N.Y.: Syracuse University Press.
Myrdal, Gunnar
  1968   *Asian Drama*. New York: Pantheon.

Wilbert R. Shenk

Nevius, John L.
  1958   *The Planting and Development of Missionary Churches.*
          Philadelphia, Pa.: Presbyterian and Reformed Publishing
          Co. (reprint).
Oosterwal, Gottfried
  1973   *Modern Messianic Movements As a Theological and Mis-
          sionary Challenge.* Scottdale, Pa.: Herald Press.
Parrinder, Geoffrey
  1963   *Witchcraft--European and African.* London: Faber and
          Faber.
Ritchie, John
  1946   *Indigenous Church Principles in Theory and Practice.* New
          York: Fleming H. Revell Co.
Rowland, Henry Hosie
  1925   *Native Churches in Foreign Fields.* Cincinnati: Methodist
          Book Concern.
Smalley, William A.
  1958   "Cultural Implications of an Indigenous Church," *Prac-
          tical Anthropology,* 5(2).
Soltau, T. S.
  1954   *Missions at the Crossroads.* Wheaton, Ill.: Van Kampen
          Press.
Soper, Edmund D.
  1943   *A Philosophy of the Christian World Mission.* New York:
          Abingdon-Cokesbury Press.
Turner, Harold W.
  1973   "Old and New Religions Among North American
          Indians," *Missiology,* I(2).
  1979   *Religious Innovation in Africa.* Boston: G. K. Hall.
  1980   "African Independent Churches and Economic Devel-
          opment," *World Development,* 8.
  1982   "The Relationship Between Development and New Reli-
          gious Movements in the Tribal Societies of the Third
          World," unpublished.
  1984   "Reflections on African Movements During a Missio-
          logical Conference," *Missionalia,* 12(3).
  1985   "New Primal Religious Movements," editorial in *Missi-
          ology,* 13(1).

Verkuyl, J.
1978   *Contemporary Missiology*. Grand Rapids: Eerdmans.

Wilbert R. Shenk

Jocelyn Murray
Mennonite Centre, London

Bibliography for Dr. Harold W. Turner

Perhaps more than for most academics, Harold Turner's bibliography closely reflects his life as it has been lived in different parts of the world and his ever-growing academic and practical interests.

Up to 1954 his home was in New Zealand, where he trained as a Presbyterian minister and eventually worked in a university hall of residence. Even in his days as a university student he was writing articles for Bible class and student magazines. Just before he left New Zealand his first book appeared, *On Halls of Residence*, and the next year OVP published an English edition.

In 1954 the whole Turner family sailed for England, and thence shortly to Freetown, Sierra Leone. The next move was to the University of Nsukka, in Nigeria. In those busy days of teaching, Harold Turner was getting to know the local congregations of African independent churches which provided the inspiration for his life's work. In 1959 he again began publishing, and from then up to the present day his output has been phenomenal, reflecting his disciplined work habits as well as his keen interest.

His early articles were largely descriptive, looking, for example, at the litany, catechism, and historical expansion of independent churches. His interest in bibliography was showing itself by 1960, and by 1963 he had already developed a typology. When we look at the dates of other studies of the Aladura and prophet churches of West Africa, we realise how important his contributions were. In 1965 came the important and innovative *Profile Through Preaching*, using sermon texts to demonstrate the sources of Aladura teachings. And in 1967 two very important works were published. There was the

Jocelyn Murray

Comprehensive Bibliography of Modern African Religious Movements (with Robert Mitchell) and the very impressive two-volume study derived from his doctoral thesis, *The History, Life and Faith of the Church of the Lord (Aladura)*.

Then came the move back to England and the University of Leicester. The bibliography now shows more attention to theoretical studies, and in 1968 a new interest, the sacred place. A short period in North America and continuing contact with his homeland of New Zealand was alerting him to the existence of religious movements parallel to those in Africa, and so the world dimension becomes apparent. But bibliography and resource materials still appear. The next move, to the University of Aberdeen, saw the setting up of the first Centre for the Study of New Religious Movements. But as a teacher of religious studies he had many other interests, and his study of Rudolf Otto, published in 1974, is still widely used by students today. In 1977 the first of the major bibliographies, that on Black Africa, was published. The bibliography on North America appeared in the next year; in 1979 a collection of his most important essays were published, along with *From Temple to Meeting House*, on the sacred place.

Retirement in formal terms makes little difference to Dr. Turner's activity but has given him more chances to travel and expand his connections. The Caribbean, Melanesia, and Australia have been added to his South Pacific, African, and North American interests. In Aberdeen and later in Birmingham he continued to read, write, and collect materials, even when, as at present, he had at last more adequate staff. This bibliography was concluded in 1989, but a number of further articles and bibliographies are still forthcoming at the date of writing. One can only suggest that the bibliography of this particular academic and innovator will never be satisfactorily brought to a neat conclusion. Now, as he returns to his homeland of New Zealand after 35 years, the wheel is coming full circle. Perhaps less on Africa may appear, but I have a feeling that a number of provincial librarians will be dusting off their newspaper archives, and that we may find some new and interesting facts about religion and mission in New Zealand and the Pacific!

Many of us, both fellow-students and colleagues, will always be grateful to Harold and to Maude for hospitality and for the help afforded us both in personal conversation and through publications and collections.

HAROLD W. TURNER BIBLIOGRAPHY
1954-1989

I. IN NEW ZEALAND, up to 1954

"Confirmation," *Scottish Journal of Theology*, 5(2), 1952, 148-162.

Halls of Residence. Wellington: New Zealand Council for Educational Research, 1953; London: Oxford University Press, 1954.

II. IN WEST AFRICA, 1955-1966

"The Litany of an Independent West African Church," *Sierra Leone Bulletin of Religion* 1 (2), 1959, 48-55; reprinted in *Practical Anthropology* 7 (6), 1960, 256-62.

"Searching and Syncretism: A West African Documentation," *International Review of Missions* 194 = 49 (April) 1960, 45-57; reprinted in *Practical Anthropology* 8 (3), 1961, 106-10.

"The Catechism of an Independent West African Church," *Sierra Leone Bulletin of Religion* 2 (2), 1960, 45-57; reprinted in *Occasional Papers* 1 (9), International Missionary Council, 1961.

"The Place of Theology in the University," in H. A. E. Sawyer (ed.), *Theology in Independent Africa*. Freetown: [University College of Freetown] 1961, 10-17.

"The Church of the Lord: The Expansion of a Nigerian Independent Church in Sierra Leone and Ghana," *Journal of African History* 3 (1), 1962, 91-110.

"The Significance of African Prophet Movements," *Hibbert Journal* 41 (3), 1963, 112-6.

Typology chart and bibliography in V.E.W. Hayward (ed.), *African Independent Church Movements*, London: Edinburgh House Press, 1963, 13, 84-94.

"The Present-Day Prophets and the Principles on Which They Work," by J. Ade Aina; a reproduction with an introduc-

tion (Materials for the Study of Nigeria and History ??).
    Nsukka, Nigeria: Crowther College of Religion, 1964.
*Profile Through Preaching: A Study of the Sermon Texts Used in a
    West African Independent Church* (C.W.M.E. Research
    Pamphlets 13). London: Edinburgh House Press, 1965.
"Pagan Features in African Independent Churches," *Practical
    Anthropology* 12 (4), 1965, 145-51.
"The Late Sir Isaac Akinyele, Olubadan of Ibadan," *West
    African Religion* 4, July 1965, 1-4.
"Prophets and Politics: A Nigerian Test Case," *Bulletin of the
    Society for African Church History* 2 (1), 1965, 97-118.
"Problems in the Study of African Independent Churches,"
    Numen 13 (1), 1966, 27-42.
"Independent Religious Groups in Eastern Nigeria," *West
    African Religion* 5 (Feb.) 1966, 7-18; *idem* 6 (Aug.) 1966,
    10-15.
"A Methodology for Modern African Religious Movements,"
    1966, *Comparative Studies in Society and History* 8 (3),
    281-294.
"Monogamy: A Mark of the Church?" *International Review of
    Missions* 219 = 55 (July) 1966, 313-21.
[With Robert C. Mitchell] *A Comprehensive Bibliography of
    Modern African Religious Movements*. Evanston, Ill.:
    Northwestern University Press, 1967.
"The Christian Version of the Sacred Place," *Reformed Liturgics*
    (Princeton, N.J.) 4 (1), 1967, 19-40.
"A Typology for Modern African Religious Movements," *Jour-
    nal of Religion and Religions* 1 (1), 1967, 1-34.
*African Independent Church: Vol. I, History of an African
    Independent Church: The Church of the Lord (Aladura);
    Vol. II, African Independent Church: The Life and Faith
    of the Church of the Lord (Aladura)*. Oxford: Clarendon
    Press, 1967.
"Theology and the University from an African Perspective,"
    Zeitschrift für Religions-und-Geistesgeschichte 19 (2),
    1967, 113-26.

III. IN LEICESTER, USA, ABERDEEN: 1968-1977

"The Phenomenology of Religion," *The Ethical Record* 73 (7), 1968, 8-10.

"The Christian Version of the Sacred Place and Its New Testament Norm," in F. L. Cross (ed.), *Studia Evangelica V, Part II*. Berlin: Akademie Verlag, 1968, 141-5.

"Bibliography of Modern African Religious Movements: Supplement I," *Journal of Religion in Africa* 1 (3), 1968, 173-210.

"African Religious Movements and Roman Catholicism," in H.-J. Greschat and H. Jungraithmayr (eds.), *Wort und Religion: Kalima na Dini* (Festschrift für Benz Ernst). Stuttgart: Evangelisches Missionsverlag, 1969, 255-64.

"The Place of Independent Religious Movements in the Modernization of Africa," *Journal of Religion in Africa* 2 (1), 1969, 43-63.

"A Model for the Structure of Religion in Relation to the Secular," *Cahiers des Religions Africaines* (Kinshasa) 3 (6), 1969, 173-97 (with French summary).

Living Tribal Religions. London: Ward Lock Educational, 1971; 2nd ed. 1973.

"Nigerien," in W. J. Hollenweger (ed.), *Die Pfingstkirchen*. Stuttgart: Evangelisches Verlag, 1971, 115-124; revised English translation, "Pentecostal Movements in Nigeria." *Orita* (Ibadan) 6 (1), 1972, 39-47.

"Bibliography of Modern African Religious Movements: Supplement II, Nos. 1602-1917," *Journal of Religion in Africa* 3 (3), 1970, 161-208.

"A Further Dimension for Missions," *International Review of Mission* 247 = 62 (July) 1973, 321-37.

"Old and New Religions Among North American Indians," *Missiology* 1 (20), 1973, 47-66.

"Patterns of Ministry and Structures Within Independent Churches in Post-Colonial Africa," in E. Fasholé-Luke, R. Gray, A. Hastings and G. O. M. Tasie (eds.), *Christianity in Independent Africa*. London: Rex Collings, 1978, 44-59.

Bibliography of New Religious Movements in Primal Societies: Vol. II: North America. Boston: G. K. Hall & Co., 1978.

"Old and New Religions in Melanesia," *Point*, no. 2 of 1978, 5-29.

Religious Innovation in Africa: Collected Essays on New Religious Movements. Boston: G. K. Hall & Co., 1979.

"The Spirituality of Independent African Churches," in *Religious Innovation in Africa*, 1979, 191-201.

From Temple to Meeting House: The Phenomenology and Theology of Places of Worship. The Hague: Mouton Publishers, 1979.

"Theological and Religious Studies in South Africa: Reflections of a Visitor," *Journal of Theology for Southern Africa* no. 30, March 1980, 3-18.

"African Independent Churches and Economic Development," *World Development* 8 (7-8), 1980, 523-33; reprinted in K. P. Jameson and C. K. Wilbur (eds.), *Religious Values and Development*. Oxford: Pergamon Press, 1981.

"Geoffrey Parrinder's Contribution to Studies of Religion in Africa," *Religion: Journal of Religion and Religions* 10 (2), 1980, 156-164.

"Caribbean Christianity" in B. E. Gates (ed.), *Afro-Caribbean Religions*. London: Ward Lock Educational, 1980, 38-48; and "New Religious Movements in the Caribbean," 49-57.

"The Way Forward in the Religious Study of African Primal Religions," *Journal of Religion in Africa* 12 (1), 1981, 1-15.

"New Vistas, Missionary and Ecumenical: Religious Movements in Primal (or Tribal) Societies," *Mission Focus* (Elkhart, Indiana), 9 (3), 1981, 45-55; reprinted in shorter form, *AACC Bulletin* (Nairobi) 12 (1), 1982, 7-18, illus.

"World of the Spirits," 128-132; "Christianity and the Primal Religions," 164; "Holy Places, Sacred Calenders," 20, in *A Lion Handbook: The World's Religions*. Tring: Lion Publishing, 1982.

"New Religious Movements in Primal Societies," in W. Flannery (ed.), *Religious Movements in Melanesia Today* (1)

(Point Series no. 2). Goroka: Melanesian Institute, 1983, 1-6.

"New Religious Movements in Primal Socicties" in J. R. Hinnells (ed.), *A Handbook of Living Religions*. New York/ Harmondsworth: Viking/Penguin Books, 1984, 439-449, 454, diagrams.

"Reflections on African Movements During a Missiological Conference," *Missionalia* 12 (3), 1984, 5-21.

"Tribal Religious Movements--New." *Encyclopaedia Britannica* (1974 ed.), vol. 18, 697-705, together with 24 briefer articles on individual movements in the Micropaedia section.

Rudolf Otto: The Idea of the Holy--A Guide for Students (with Introduction to the Man, by P. R. McKenzie). Aberdeen: printed for the author, 1974.

"The Contribution of Studies on Religion in Africa to Western Religious Studies" in M. E. Glasswell and E. W. Fasholé-Luke (eds.), *New Testament Christianity for Africa and the World: Essays in Honour of Harry Sawyerr*. London: S.P.C.K., 1974, 169-78.

"New Religious Movements Among Primal Peoples: Repercussions of the Christian Contact," *Milligan Missiogram* (Milligan College, Tennessee) 2 (1), 1974, 13-16.

"African Independent Churches and Education," *Journal of Modern African Studies* 13 (2), 1975, 295-308.

"New Religious Movements in the Primal Societies," *World Faiths* (London), no. 95, 1975, 5-10.

"A New Field in the History of Religion," *Journal of Religion and Religions*, 1(1), Spring 1971, 15-23.

"The Study of New Religious Movements in Africa, 1968-75," *Religion: A Journal of Religion and Religions* 6 (1), 1976, 88-98.

Bibliography of New Religious Movements in Primal Societies: Vol. I: Black Africa. Boston: G. K. Hall & Co., 1977.

"The Approach to Africa's Religious Movements," *African Perspectives* (Leiden; formerly *Kroniek van Afrika*) 6 (2), 1976/77, 13-23.

"Eglises independantes d'origine et de formes africaines," *Concilium: Revue internationale de théologie*, no. 126, juin 1977, 133-140.

"Primal Religions and Their Study," in V. C. Hayes (ed.), *Australian Essays in World Religions*. Adelaide; Australian Association for the Study of Religions, 1977, 27-37; also "New Religious Movements in Primal Societies," 38-48.

IV. RETIREMENT, ABERDEEN AND BIRMINGHAM, from 1978

"Understanding the New World of Religious Movements in Primal Societies," *Expository Times* 89 (6), 1978, 167-72.

"The Hidden Power of the Whites: The Secret Religion Withheld from the Primal Peoples," *Archives de Sciences Sociales des Religion* no. 46 (1), 1978, 41-55.

"A Further Frontier for Missions," *Missionalia* 11 (3), 1983, 103-112; reprinted in Gaba Reprints, 1984.

"And Brought Forth Fruit an Hundredfold: Sharing Western Documentary Resources with the Third World by Microfiche," *International Bulletin of Missionary Research* 9 (3), 1985, 110-114.

"New Mission Task: Worldwide and Waiting," *Missiology* 13 (1), 1985, 5-21; ibid., "Bibliography on NERMS," 103-110; "Centre for New Religious Movements," 117-119.

"The Relationship Between Development and New Religious Movements in the Tribal Societies of the Third World," in F. Ferre and R. H. Mataragnon (eds.), *God and Global Justice: Religion and Poverty in an Unequal World*. New York: Paragon House, 1985, 84-110; reprinted as "Tradition and Change in Africa" in *The World and I* (Washington D.C.) 1 (1), 1986, 246-261.

"Andrew Walls as Scholar," in James Thrower (ed.), *Essays in Religious Studies for Andrew Walls*. University of Aberdeen, Department of Religious Studies, 1986, 1-4.

"Articulating Theology Through Relations with New Religious Movements," *Discernment* (London, B.C.) 1 (2), 1986, 4-15.

"A Global Phenomenon," in *New Religious Movements and the Churches*. Geneva: World Council of Churches Publications, 1987, 3-15.

"The New Religious Movements as Free Partners in a Plural Society," in H. O. Thompson (ed.), *Global Outreach: Global Congress of the World's Religions*. Barrytown: Unification Theological Church Seminary, 1987, 4-12.

"New Religious Movements Related to Primal Religions" in A. Brown (gen. ed.), *The SHAP Handbook on World Religions in Education*. London: Commission on Racial Equality, and SHAP Working Party on World Religions in Education, 1987, 97-98.

"Rastafari--A Bibliographical Paper," *The SHAP Handbook on World Religions in Education*. London: Commission on Racial Equality, 1987, 162.

"Prolegomena to a Conference on Ministry to African Independent Churches," in David A. Shank (ed.) *Ministry of Missions to African Independent Churches*. Elkhart, Indiana: Mennonite Board of Missions, 1987, 4-12. See also Appendix A, "New Mission Task: Worldwide and Waiting," reprinted from *Missiology* 13 (1), 1985, 243-259.

"The Human and the Spiritual," *Selly Oak Journal*, no. 8, Spring 1988, 16-23.

"New Religious Movements and the Law in Britain." *Quaderni di diritto e politica ecclesiastica*. Padua: Casa a Ed. Antonio Milani, 1988, 48-49.

"New Religious Movements--Africa," in *The World's Religions*, ed. by Stewart Sutherland, Peter Clarke et al. London: Routledge, 1988, 945-952.

"Nouveaux mouvements religieux et cultures tribales," in *Encyclopedia Universalis: le grand atlas des religions*, 1988, 140-141.

"My Pilgrimage in Mission," *International Bulletin of Missionary Research* 13 (2), April 1989, 71-74.